The Living Word

Also by Harold Klemp

Ask the Master, Book 1
Ask the Master, Book 2
Child in the Wilderness
The Living Word, Book 1
Soul Travelers of the Far Country
The Spiritual Exercises of ECK
The Temple of ECK
The Wind of Change

The Mahanta Transcripts Series

Journey of Soul, Book 1
How to Find God, Book 2
The Secret Teachings, Book 3
The Golden Heart, Book 4
Cloak of Consciousness, Book 5
Unlocking the Puzzle Box, Book 6
The Eternal Dreamer, Book 7
The Dream Master, Book 8
We Come as Eagles, Book 9
The Drumbeat of Time, Book 10
What Is Spiritual Freedom? Book 11
How the Inner Master Works, Book 12

Stories to Help You See God in Your Life

The Book of ECK Parables, Volume 1
The Book of ECK Parables, Volume 2
The Book of ECK Parables, Volume 3
The Book of ECK Parables, Volume 4

MAHANTA

This book has been authored by and published under the supervision of the Mahanta, the Living ECK Master, Sri Harold Klemp. It is the Word of ECK.

The Living Word

Book 2

Harold Klemp

ECKANKAR
Minneapolis, MN

The Living Word, Book 2

Printed in U.S.A.

Compiled by Mary Carroll Moore
Edited by Joan Klemp and Anthony Moore

Text illustrations by Fraser MacDonald
Back cover photo by Robert Huntley

Publisher's Cataloging-in-Publication
(Prepared by Quality Books Inc.)

Klemp, Harold.
  The living word. Book 2 / Harold Klemp.
  p. cm.
  Includes index.
  ISBN 1-57043-115-9

  1. Eckankar (Organization)—Doctrines. I. Title.

BP605.E3K54 1996   299'.93
                                     QBI96-20271

Contents

Foreword

The teachings of ECK define the nature of Soul. You are Soul, a particle of God sent into the worlds (including earth) to gain spiritual experience.

The goal in ECK is spiritual freedom in this lifetime, after which you become a Co-worker with God, both here and in the next world. Karma and reincarnation are primary beliefs.

Key to the ECK teachings is the Mahanta, the Living ECK Master. He has the special ability to act as both the Inner and Outer Master for ECK students. He is the prophet of Eckankar, given respect but not worship. He teaches the sacred name of God, HU, which lifts you spiritually into the Light and Sound of God, the ECK. Purified by the practice of the Spiritual Exercises of ECK, you are then able to accept the full love of God in this lifetime.

Sri Harold Klemp is the Mahanta, the Living ECK Master. He has written many books, discourses, and articles about the spiritual life. Many of his public talks are available on audio- and videocassette. His teachings uplift people and help them recognize and understand their own experiences in the Light and Sound of God.

The Living Word, Book 2, is a collection of articles

by Sri Harold from 1989 to 1995. If you uncover only a tenth of the spiritual truth and divine love within these pages, you'll be transformed into a nobler state of being, many times over.

The word *HU,* an ancient name for God, descends from the highest spiritual realms. It is a word people anywhere can use to address the Originator of Life. It uplifts and purifies us, heals our wounds, soothes our brow: Sweet, but mighty, name of God.

1

HU, the Age-Old Name for God

People have given many names to the Deity. Better known to Western society are Zeus of ancient Greece, Jupiter of the Romans, Odin of Norse mythology, and Aton of the early Egyptian civilization. Equally important in history are Ahura Mazda ("God of Light") of the Persians, Brahma of the Hindu sacred trinity, Elohim of the Jewish religion, and Allah of the Muslims.

Perhaps least known among the many names is HU, the universal name for God. The brotherhood of ECK Adepts has known of it for centuries. The spiritual hierarchy picked the present age to bring knowledge of it to the modern world.

HU is both a name for God and a sound of the Audible Life Stream, which we know as the ECK, or Holy Spirit. HU, along with Sugmad, is a charged name for God that can spiritually uplift the people of any religion.

People glimpse a quality of the Supreme Deity and fit a name to their concept of the All-in-the-All in their native tongue. Despite the many names for God, none is God. It exists alone and supreme, beyond the grasp

1

of the human mind. God exists in and of Itself.

In ECK, we do know this: HU is foremost among the ancient names for God. It is the true, universal name drawn from the Sound Current Itself, for HU is woven into the language of life. It is the Sound of all sounds. It is the wind in the leaves, falling rain, thunder of jets, singing of birds, the awful rumble of a tornado. Again, Its sound is heard in laughter, weeping, the din of city traffic, ocean waves, and the quiet rippling of a mountain stream. And yet, the word *HU* is not God. It is a word people anywhere can use to address the Originator of Life.

The word *HU* descends from the highest spiritual realms. It springs from the tenth plane, the Nameless World.

The Shariyat-Ki-Sugmad, Way of the Eternal, says of the sacred sound HU: "In this mantric sound all the positive and forward-pressing forces of the human, which are trying to blow up its limitations and burst the fetters of ignorance, are united and concentrated on the ECK, like an arrow point."

HU, adds *The Shariyat,* is the way out of "personal misery of every kind; out of the meaninglessness of life; out of boredom, discouragement, failure, obsessive anxiety, or depression; and out of fear."

Every religion ever created by ECK was to breathe new life into the spiritual evolution of the human race. This is true of animism (a spirit in every object), polytheism (many gods of different standing), dualism (equal forces of good and evil), or monotheism (a religion governed by a single God).

All religions are of ECK. All, especially in the beginning, provide their followers with a new understanding of life. The development of each religion sees the rise of leaders who reshape and structure the

2

original teachings to fit the changing times.

Therefore, records left by past religious writers still bear a message for us today. In Christianity, early church fathers grappled with the nature of God, Soul, truth, angels, and heaven.

Was God almighty? If so, what explained the existence of Satan?

How many angels could dance on the head of a pin? Was this question driven by idle curiosity, or were the church fathers searching for an Achilles' heel of Soul? Might angels, good or evil, be of such fine substance as to penetrate the shell of Soul? If Soul's defenses were so exposed to an outside influence, even that of an angel, did this restrict one's free will? Could this alter Soul's quest for salvation?

Questions like these have churned the dust since mankind's arrival on earth. In each succeeding age, humanity has developed a rash of ideas about what God is and what God is not. Yet, all remains in the realm of opinion.

Not a single church father from orthodox religion has been able to tell his people: "This is what God is!" and be right about it. He *believes* he knows the true spiritual relationship that exists between God and the individual, but his is also only an untried opinion.

In this lies the strength of Eckankar. It also comes to people with a message about the divine mysteries. Yet how it passes along this knowledge is beyond anything ever found in the teachings of any orthodox religion. Its ultimate authority rests not with a personality, not even with that of the Mahanta, the Living ECK Master. Its authority is HU, the universal name for God.

This word has a spiritual force that speaks volumes by itself. It has little need for a human agent, except for the Light Giver. He is the Mahanta, who links Soul with the Sound Current. He helps each find spiritual freedom by passing along this forgotten, holy name of God.

The word is HU. It depends upon no human authority for validation. No priest, minister, or spiritual figure can say HU is this or that. It is what it is. From a practical standpoint, it is love's golden thread, drawing Soul closer to God, like an infant to its parent.

HU is a love song to God. It uplifts and purifies us of the evils that make life too much to bear. It heals our wounds, soothes our brow: sweet, but mighty, name of God.

In all heaven and earth no name is mightier than HU. It can lift the grieving heart to a temple of solace. A companion in trouble, it is likewise a friend in times of prosperity. And is it any wonder, for HU is Soul's most precious gift from God.

Anytime you sing HU as a love offering to Sugmad, the Lord of all creation, your heart fills with the Light and Sound of God. They are the twin aspects of ECK, the Holy Spirit. HU, the name of God, brings us into a holy alliance with the Light and Sound, the Word of God. Should the worlds tremble and all else fail, HU carries us into the ocean of God's love and mercy.

So sing HU softly, gently. Once among the most secret names of God, the Order of Vairagi Adepts has now brought it into the world for the upliftment of all. It is for those who desire true love, true freedom, wisdom, and truth.

In time, people everywhere will have the chance to sing this age-old, universal name for God. This is a new cycle in the spiritual history of the human community.

It will all be due to HU.

4

Try this spiritual exercise to hear and see the two aspects of God, the Light and Sound. Sit or lie down, put your attention on your Spiritual Eye, and sing, "Show me thy ways, O Lord."

2

In Pursuit of God

The window from where I write looks out into our backyard, which borders a small grove of trees. My wife and I call it "the forest."

This forest is home to our family of animals: a chipmunk, some red foxes that drop by in search of a meal, Mr. and Mrs. Stretch Rabbit, and a tree full of squirrels. All, even the foxes at times, come to eat birdseed from two feeding dishes set out for them.

The squirrels are the most fun to watch. Two large squirrels hog the feeding dishes by sitting down in them, chasing away lesser members of the family who must get by with old seed on the ground. After eating, the family retires to the forest to relax and play.

Yet life is not a paradise. To spoil this happy scene, a neighbor's brown-and-white dog races by on occasion to chase the birds and animals at the dishes. But they always manage to flee in time.

Then, a few weeks ago, I saw what looked like a newcomer to our family: a small rabbit with short ears. It left a dish of birdseed and hopped toward a tall tree in the forest. Idly, I watched. To my surprise, this one didn't run around the tree like a normal rabbit. Instead, he ran straight up the trunk.

What a marvelous trick!

Of course, this very curious animal was only a squirrel who'd traded his tail for his life, much to the chagrin of his pursuer. We now call that squirrel Lucky.

* * *

Many people in pursuit of God are like the birds and animals in our backyard. In fact, they are like Lucky. Gorging on food and drink, they trip off to play in the forest, returning to the feeding dish each day for more of the same. And life rolls merrily on. Then one day, a complication comes to steal a prized possession, like Lucky's handsome tail.

And life is nevermore the same.

But it goes on.

* * *

A search for happiness is the pursuit of God. Yet the reason so many people fail to find happiness is because they look for it in the wrong place—at the market instead of in their hearts.

It takes discipline to pursue God.

There is no mystery to finding God: just follow the Sound of the Divine Voice back home. Could anything be easier? Not so for most people, for whom the pursuit of God is as unlikely as the phenomenon of a flying rabbit. And why? It's simply not in their consciousness yet to know that the destiny of each Soul is to become a Co-worker with God, who expects more of us than an eternity of eating and play.

For many, life is much like a trip to a casino. They place all their talents and dreams on the gaming table then bet the outcome of this life upon a turn of the wheel of fortune. That is the sum of their spiritual life in pursuit of God.

Happiness, to them, is blind luck.

Yet some individuals do have a true desire for God and use some form of prayer or worship to better understand the Creator. Mostly, however, their prayer is like traffic on a one-way street: They do all the talking. It never occurs to them to stop for a moment and listen. God may want to speak.

Often, God doesn't get a word in at all.

How, then, does God communicate with us?

Every student of ECK knows that God speaks to all life with the voice of divine Light and Sound. The Christian name for these dual aspects of God is the Holy Spirit, or the Holy Ghost, which we in Eckankar refer to by the age-old name ECK.

The range of vibration in the universe spans from infinity to infinity. And while the primal cause of vibration is the Light and Sound of God, the human voice is a mere speck on the full scale of vibration. Why would God only speak in a whisper? Yet people who believe that God speaks chiefly in the frequency range of the human voice forget that the human voice, in comparison to the universe of sound, is but a tiny whisper.

So the idea that God only speaks to life within the narrow field of human sound is an attempt to reduce the might of God.

The Light and Sound of God are the food and drink of saints. Do you need the reminder of Saul of Tarsus on the road to Damascus—struck to the earth by the Light of God? Martin Luther, the great reformer, was also fortunate to see It. Then there was Genghis Khan, the Mongol conqueror of the thirteenth century, who every so often would fall into a swoon for days, able only to chant HU, an ancient name for God. In those trance states, he saw and heard the majestic Light and

Sound of God. The Divine One spoke through the Holy Spirit.

So the highest form of speech from God to the more spiritually advanced of the human race is the Light and Sound.

Who, then, does God talk to?

In fact, everyone who has made a contribution to the human race has heard or seen the True Voice. The ways of God are many. God often speaks in a less direct manner to dreamers, poets, visionaries, and prophets. It speaks to people, in part, through visions or dreams, daydreams, prayer (the listening kind), or intuition.

History tells of many such people.

A list of famous people who have been a mouthpiece for the Voice of God includes the likes of Socrates, Plato, Elijah, King David, Mozart, Beethoven, Jung, Einstein, Shelley, Edison, Michelangelo, and thousands more. Each does his best to render the divine will into human terms, using a natural genius as the tool of communication.

The Sound and Light carry out God's scheme of creation. So the highest anyone can aspire to is a life of high creativity, but always guided by the force of divine love.

That is how to be most like God.

* * *

Try this simple spiritual exercise to help you hear and see the two aspects of God, the Light and Sound.

Go somewhere quiet. Sit or lie down in a comfortable place. Put your attention on your Spiritual Eye, a point just above and behind your eyebrows. With eyes lightly shut, begin to sing a holy word or phrase, such as HU, God, Holy Spirit, or "Show me thy ways, O Lord." But fill your heart with love before you approach the altar of God, because only the pure may come.

Be patient. Do this exercise for several weeks, for a limit of twenty minutes each time. Sit, sing, and wait. God speaks only when you are able to listen.

There is more to the pursuit of God than luck.

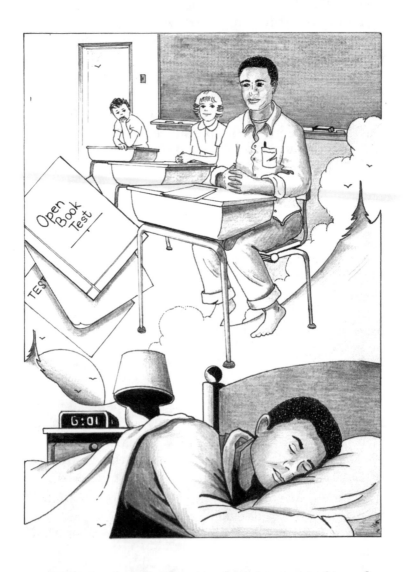

Dreams can tell a dreamer how in or out of tune he
is with the Light and Sound—and thus, with himself.
One night Jerry had a dream in which he was a student again.

3

Your Universe of Dreams

How can I feel close to God?

Millions of people, from the earliest days of man, have asked questions like this during times of personal anguish. Who has the answer?

For many, it is the Mahanta, the Living ECK Master. Spiritual guide for thousands around the world, he says, "Your daily experience is but a drop in the ocean of life. What do you know about your universe of dreams?"

Some religious leaders set social or political goals for their followers. However, the Mahanta comes to show people the real purpose for living. "The experience of life," he says, "is to lead you to the awareness of God." He shows you how to live the best life possible.

Through dreams and other means, the Mahanta introduces people of every religion to the Sound and Light of God. Most individuals do not know what they are.

What universal force operates in the background to establish harmony in our lives? It is the ECK, otherwise known as the Life Stream of God, the Audible Sound Current, Holy Spirit, the Heavenly Music,

Sanctifier, Bani, Music of the Spheres—and as the Light and Sound of God. These are among the many ways throughout history that people have spoken of the Voice of God.

How does one find these two aspects of the Voice of God? Usually, it starts with dreams. The pathway to the Light and Sound includes: (1) *belief* in ECK, the seedbed of unfoldment; (2) *experience,* the cultivator; and (3) *awareness,* the harvest.

Dreams, as a tool of awareness, can tell a dreamer how in or out of tune he is with the Light and Sound— and thus, with himself. For example, let's look at a businessman named Jerry. His productivity at work had slipped because of his unsystematic habits. As a result, he was unhappy, blaming his family and associates when things went wrong.

One night he had a dream in which he was a student again. His instructor had given him and his classmates an open-book test to do at home. They were to turn it in for grading at the next class period.

At home, Jerry answered most of the questions before mislaying the test among a stack of other papers on his desk. He found it, but just before class the next morning, he discovered he had made a mistake: Somehow he had put his answers on someone else's test paper. By then it was too late to complete his own test, so he decided to stay home and be absent from class.

After class, a classmate told him that the instructor had graded the students' tests but had then given a second test. Suddenly, Jerry was two tests behind. Troubled, he awoke.

What did his dream mean?

The instructor was the Mahanta, spiritual guide for ECK initiates. The Mahanta, like a teacher, sets

14

a program of spiritual study for everyone in Eckankar. This study, which involves every aspect of a person's life, may be partly reflected in his dreams.

The dream showed Jerry filling out someone else's test paper in error. At his office in the physical world, Jerry often let others convince him to help with their work, but at the expense of his own. That was clearly a mistake. His classmates in the dream represented a spiritual standard, which he might reach with a minimum of effort. To regain harmony with the spiritual standard of ECK, he needed to set new priorities at the office.

His dream gave an important principle: "Life goes forward. Keep up or fall behind." This was shown by the teacher grading the tests of Jerry's classmates, while giving them another test during the same class. Because of Jerry's absence, he was immediately two tests behind. That added up to a widening gap between him and Divine Spirit.

In a capsule, this dream was warning: "You're out of tune with life. Get back in step!" Once he set new priorities, his discontent vanished.

Dreams, visions, and other experiences mean nothing in themselves. But in the context of our spiritual life, they are signs of how much we are in accord with life. In fact, the whole point of life is to teach us how to come into agreement with the Voice of God, the Light and Sound. Many find the road to their inner worlds through the teachings of Eckankar. Often, however, it takes a personal tragedy to drive us in search of the meaning of life.

A mother, very close to her son, found Eckankar after his death in a motorcycle accident. Devastated by her loss, she was unable to find comfort at church. She regularly cried through the entire service. If only she could feel closer to God, then maybe He would help her understand why the accident occurred. More important, where was her son now? Was he all right? She prayed for help constantly.

Five months later, while at her lowest ebb, she had an experience that changed her life. At first, she thought it was a dream, but it was actually Soul Travel.

The mother awoke in vivid consciousness in the other worlds. A bespectacled woman with grey streaks in her dark hair met the mother, and they talked for a few minutes. "Do you know my son?" she asked the woman, giving his name.

"Of course I know him," said the woman. "He lives right over there in that white house." The scene was a normal setting of cottages, such as near a lake resort.

The mother and her son had a long conversation. He assured her that his health was better than it had been on earth. Then he looked at her and said, "I know what you're doing to yourself. Please stop. You're hurting yourself." Before they parted, she asked if she could hold him in her arms, since she didn't get a chance to do so before his death. Laughing, he said, "OK, Mom." Soul Travel put her right there with him. She could feel him in her arms. Then she awoke.

His scent still lingered with her, and a peaceful, happy feeling lasted for weeks before it began to fade.

She was now determined to find out where he was. Somewhere on earth, she knew, somebody had the answer. That's when her sister introduced her to Eckankar. The first book she read was *The Spiritual Notebook*. It convinced her that here was the answer to her prayers. Here was an explanation that actually made sense.

Grief for her son still overtakes her on occasion. She wants the Mahanta, the Living ECK Master to help her regain the peace she felt with her son during Soul Travel. She does the Spiritual Exercises of ECK daily. They are in *The ECK Dream Discourses,* which come with membership in Eckankar. She now directs her efforts toward seeing the Light and hearing the Sound—keys to the secret worlds of God.

Stories like this may inspire one to look for truth and love, but finding them depends upon doing the right thing. For those in ECK, it is doing the spiritual exercises.

The spiritual exercises are in the ECK books and discourses, and take twenty to thirty minutes a day. They are simply a love song to God or a conversation with Divine Spirit that can help you find a new appreciation for life. Many ECKists develop their own spiritual exercises, once they catch the knack from the ECK teachings.

Here's an easy spiritual exercise called "The Blue Curtain of God." The first part awakens the seeing power of Soul. Find a time to sit or lie down for ten to twenty minutes when you will not be disturbed. Shut your eyes, but imagine you are gently looking at a dark blue curtain on the wall before you. The first few days, expect to see only the rich blue curtain. Sooner or later, some color of the Light of God will shine from it.

The second part of the spiritual exercise attunes your spiritual hearing. While looking at the blue curtain, begin to sing softly the word *HU* (pronounced like the word *hue*). HU is an old name for God used by saints for thousands of years. After a few minutes, sing HU within yourself, making no audible sound. Continue singing for a few minutes more until you wish to stop. Then sit quietly, still looking at the rich blue curtain before you.

One more thing: Throughout this short exercise, carry in your heart a feeling of love for God.

When you finish your devotion, go about your day as usual. Then at bedtime, think briefly of the blue curtain and the word *HU*. Quietly, to yourself, say, "Show me Thy will, O God. Teach me to love Thee."

Over the next few days, try to remember your dreams. No matter how inconsequential they may seem, write down any images to jog your memory for contemplation later. The Mahanta or the Holy Spirit will use dreams to give you special guidance and understanding.

Spend time in your universe of dreams. You will find the grace of more insight, harmony, and joy in your spiritual life.

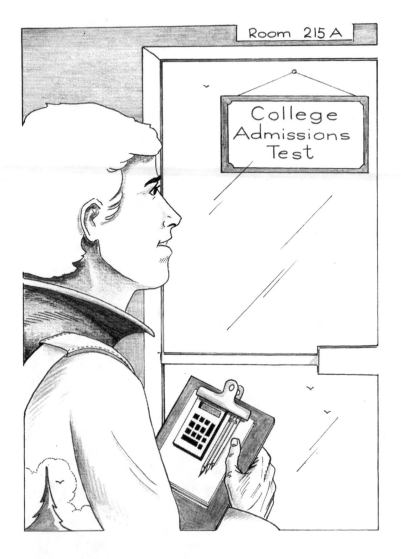

The right way to take control of your own life is to put everything into the hands of Divine Spirit, then go about your daily life and do everything in the name of God.

4

Your Superstitions—
How They Put You in a Box

None of us is superstitious. Just ask and we'll swear to it (though with fingers crossed for luck, of course).

So then why do other people have superstitions?

Alvin Schwartz thinks he knows the reason. Author of *Cross Your Fingers, Spit in Your Hat,* Schwartz says: "When we are faced with situations we cannot control—which depend on luck or chance—superstitions make us feel more secure." He adds that many are also funny and give us pleasure: "the stuff of which hopes and dreams are made."

And yet, if you have superstitions, they do put you in a box spiritually. It's as Schwartz said: They make us feel more secure in situations where we have no control. The trouble is, they don't help. All you've done is give up the control of your life to a ritual whose only power is to make you more dependent upon it. Each time you cross your fingers or spit in your hat for luck, you put just another barrier between the ECK (Holy Spirit) and you. And can superstition ever free you from fear?

What are some pet superstitions of other people?

21

For example, did you ever see wedding guests throw rice at a bridegroom and bride? Since rice is so plentiful, it was to wish the newlyweds a happy marriage with many children and much food. The ritual of throwing rice was to give a sense of control to life, where there is often little.

The bride's veil was originally to hide her face from evil spirits, who hated weddings and would do anything to make trouble. If a rival turned up at the wedding, the veil also protected the bride from the evil eye, which could "harm or kill a person, an animal, or a plant with a single glance." A bride was an easy target. Of course, *we* don't go in for such nonsense.

But say a mirror breaks. How does a person avoid seven years of bad luck? The simplest way, says Schwartz, is to wait seven hours before cleaning up the mess. He explains the reason behind this belief: "When early man saw his reflection in a pond or a lake, he thought what he saw was part of him. And when the wind rippled the water and shattered his image, he was sure he also would have trouble. This is how men later felt when they broke a mirror that once held their image."

And if you believe in bad luck, you'll always be very careful what you do with salt. You won't waste it, spill it, give it away, or even be so foolish as to hand anyone a salt shaker. You'll carefully set it down in front of the other person. Let him take the risk of spilling it. You just can't be too careful.

Why such care with salt?

Before the age of the refrigerator, people used salt to keep their food from going bad and giving them food poisoning. Salt was thus a way to stave off death. It also became a precious commodity, used even as money. If a person happened to spill and waste some, he took it as a sign that evil spirits were hanging about, trying to cause him ill. To ward them off, he would quickly toss a pinch of salt over his left shoulder to where they lurk. So now you know.

Now imagine that you and a friend take a walk, and a post or a bush separates you. Some say that it could cause your friend and you to quarrel, unless you both say at once, "Salt and pepper!" You may also say, "Bread and butter," but you'd better say it together.

There is also the small matter of New Year's Eve celebrations. Do you ever recall being at such a party and joining the other guests to make the most awful din at the stroke of midnight? Why? Was it to welcome in the New Year? Perhaps it was a way of trying to chase away evil spirits and insure good fortune for yourself in the coming year. Even if you no longer help create bedlam on New Year's Eve, that is why people began the practice long ago. Now it's only a custom.

Let's say, though, you're the odd one: You won't make noise to usher in the New Year. But if I should sneeze, you would say, "Bless you" or "Gesundheit," and I would thank you for the kindness.

That simple gesture of social courtesy also grew out of a superstition. A sneeze could be a very serious matter, because people once believed that a person's spirit was part of his breath and he might sneeze his life away. Worse, if he opened his mouth, evil spirits might enter his body; or if already there, a sneeze could blast them out to attack others. A sneeze was no laughing matter.

What's the spiritual point to all this? The right way to take control of your own life is to put everything into the hands of Divine Spirit, then go about your daily life and do everything in the name of God. Forget about horseshoes, a lucky rabbit's foot, or wishing upon a star.

How do you let the Spirit of God into your life? The simplest and best way is to sing HU, the age-old song of love for God. It's just one word, and you sing it as the word *hue*—in one long, steady note. HU will put a fresh, new spirit into your life. You will begin to be a happier person, because It will show you what things are truly important for you and what are not.

You need never cross your fingers or spit in your hat for luck again. You have HU, which is greater by far.

Life connects. The events in our lives are diamonds, and invisible lines run between them. To be happy, we must take the initiative to connect those points that bring love and goodness to us.

5

Connecting Diamonds

Why do people often appear to fail? This question has bothered me a long time, simply because so many people are unhappy with their lot. What can they do to improve their lives?

There is a spiritual principle called Connecting Diamonds that is at work every day of our lives, whether we are aware of it or not. Be forewarned, it's not a shortcut. And that is perhaps why so many of us overlook this principle, and even do everything in our power to resist it.

Let's look at an example:

An old friend of an ECKist came to town for a visit. The two decided to find a billiard parlor and enjoy an afternoon of billiards. They looked in the phone directory, found the location of a few places, then set out for one. Although they had agreed to try the first place on their list, the driver was actually en route to the second location before either noticed the error. So they turned around. To save time, and with map in hand, they took a shortcut along some unfamiliar streets. Soon they reached their destination. But the billiard tables were all full, which meant either waiting for a table or else trying to find another parlor with an open table. So they left.

They climbed back into the car, checked the map, then set out for the second choice on their list—a location many miles distant, on the other side of town.

By an odd coincidence, the second place happened to be on the very same street. However, this fact was not apparent to them as they drove, because their route ran along city streets, onto a freeway, then back onto city streets again. But this second billiard parlor, which the driver had instinctively set out for at the start, was on the same street as the first, although many miles apart.

That is an example of connecting diamonds.

It works like this: We perceive of some idea that we feel will enrich our life at that very moment. We make a plan. Then we set out from home to accomplish the first leg of our search, but find the ECK is actually trying to get us to go directly to the second place. We resist the guidance of the Holy Spirit. We check our original plans (road map) again and try to find a shortcut to the place we think we should be at. When we arrive, nothing works out.

The trip is not a loss, however, unless we become discouraged and head straight home.

But giving up is too easy. If, instead, we decide to pursue our original plan, we will bring out the map again and try to find a new route to our destination. In doing so, we often find that a line connects all the main points in our quest. Individuals who know and follow this principle of connecting diamonds are usually happy and successful in life.

Those who are always unhappy are also those who give up too soon on ECK.

We are talking here about the ECK-Vidya, the

ancient science of prophecy. Every event in our life is part of a divine plan that accounts for each so-called mistake or happening of chance. Most people don't know that life connects. They don't realize that the events in their lives are diamonds and that invisible lines run between them in every possible direction and combination of points. To be happy, we must take the initiative to connect those points that bring love and goodness to us.

How do you start?

You cannot ever put too much emphasis upon having a spiritual frame of mind. So begin every day with the Spiritual Exercises of ECK. Sing HU or your personal word. The spiritual exercises will give you the strongest connection of all—a bond with the ECK, the Holy Spirit.

Second, sit back and dream the sort of life you would like. What would you like to do? To be? Think backward from the goal of your desire. That will be your plan for achievement.

Third, begin.

That's looking at your plan for spiritual happiness and success from end to beginning. Now let's look at it more logically. There will be three stages, or connecting diamonds, to this plan. First, you must do something, or make a beginning. But where? In what direction? Until you know the third, or final, point of the connecting diamonds (your goal), you cannot begin to work toward that end. So see a picture of your goal.

You'll notice that an uncomfortable space still lies between step one, the starting point, and the third step, your goal. This middle point is the unformed, creative part where the Holy Spirit works Its wonders to help you accomplish what you cannot do yourself.

How do you get moving?

You'll never get to this miraculous part of life until you set a goal. Then you must take the initiative and begin to move toward it. Only then will the Holy Spirit help you through the large, unknown second area, where you must exercise your talents to create a better life for yourself.

Paul Twitchell speaks about the diamond. In *The ECK-Vidya, Ancient Science of Prophecy,* he says: "The diamond . . . is related to the physical world and man's human experience. It represents divine power brought to bear upon the material conditions. Intuition, clairvoyance, inspiration are faculties of the higher mind whereby light is reflected as from a flawless diamond."

Do you want to be happy? Then set out to learn about the connecting diamonds in your own life. They shimmer and glisten all around you.

But always begin your search by singing HU, or some other love song to God.

Dreams are a direct line to the sea of our hidden life, much like a fishing line dropped from a small boat into a bottomless sea. Our memory of dreams is a glimpse of the full spiritual life that each of us leads beyond the physical.

6

Your Dreams
and Graceful Living

Dreams are a direct line to the sea of our hidden life, much like a fishing line dropped from a small boat into a bottomless sea.

A person who learns to dream well can usually take everyday life in stride, because dreams give him or her a perception that others cannot help but notice. An understanding of dreams can steady us for the surprises of the day, and so aid us in learning to manage stress with more foresight and grace.

Dreams often tell what's coming.

A friend from the Air Force and I keep in touch with an exchange of letters every few months. Usually, he comes for a visit on the inner planes while writing me a letter. Next morning, I'll tell my wife about our visit on the inner planes.

"Ray must be writing a letter again," I say.

And it usually comes a few days later.

Dreams are like that fishing line dropped from a boat into the sea. They are much more than a communication link, which the line suggests: Our memory of dreams is a glimpse of the full spiritual life that each of us leads beyond the physical. Our daily physical life has as little scope or variety as might exist in a rowboat. A full spiritual life, on the other hand, includes all events around the boat (human self), including those within the sea, on the land, and in the sky of existence.

Dreams are a large part of each person's hidden life, and it's this sea of experience that we want to look at.

Sue (not her real name) went through a divorce and other problems that brought on a weariness of living. In the past, at the height of distress, she often had a series of troubling, recurring dreams about the last days of school, usually just before final exams. She could not stomach the thought of having to deal with a single day more of classes. It was easier to skip them. The next morning, Sue would awaken with a deep loathing for the problems of living.

Then the realization struck her: She just wanted to go home to God. Weary of the lessons of life, she was tired of having to face still another boring lesson, a repeat of a spiritual law she had refused to learn in the past.

These she called her quitter's dreams.

Through ECK, Sue has come to understand that life on earth is like an academy, a camp of discipline where people learn the laws of Divine Spirit (ECK). In her case, the ECK is cleaning out old wounds and pouring Its healing Light and Sound into the dark, infected areas of karma in her life. The emotional pain she so often feels is from her resistance to the changes of Divine Spirit. As the pain of daily life drives itself deeper into her, she nevertheless feels the love behind it opening her heart wider to God.

When she remembers to look at herself in a spiritual light, she sees the deep capacity for love this pain has brought her. The realization fills her with wonder. Now she can rise in the morning and greet the new day with grace and wonder.

Another sort of dream may tell a dreamer where to look for an actual treasure. Yet the real experience may be a test of spiritual grace.

A young woman and her husband moved from a small, crowded apartment into a house her father owned. Shortly before moving day, she had two separate dreams that told of money hidden somewhere in their new home. Busy with the move, she set the dreams aside.

When it was time to connect the gas for heating and cooking, she called the utility company, which sent a serviceman. He checked all the appliances that used gas and found a paper bag hidden behind an old oven.

"Do you want this paper bag?" he asked the young woman. "It could catch fire back here."

Remembering her two dreams, she quickly replied, "Yes, give it to me, please." Casually, she placed it on the kitchen table, in full view, though in her heart she suspected it was full of money. After the serviceman had left, she opened the bag and indeed found a large wad of bills.

Yet this house was the property of her father. Instead of saying "Finders keepers," she put the cash in a safe place for her father, who was out of town for the weekend. Upon his return, she gave him the full amount, for it had never occurred to her to keep any for herself. He, in turn, let her keep it all—in appreciation for her love, grace, and honesty.

This young woman did profit from her dream. When the serviceman had handed her the bag, she took it calmly and placed it on the kitchen table in plain sight—as if it were of no value. This calmed suspicion and any chance that he might tell others about her good fortune, only later to have someone try to break in and steal it. Told in her dreams about the contents of the paper bag, she could act wisely and safeguard it for her father, the real owner.

A dreamer lives in many worlds at once. And yes, dreams do enrich life.

You can learn more about your dream life by reading ECK books on the subject, like *The Eternal Dreamer*. Also available to new members of ECK are the ECK dream discourses.

Dreams are a spiritual tool of the Holy Spirit to help you find your way to God. Take advantage of this help. There is so much more to life than you'll ever find in something so small as a rowboat, or as narrow as the human state of consciousness.

A study of dreams the ECK way can help you enter a more productive, calm, and graceful life.

Whenever you have a dream, jot it down in a notebook. Write down your feelings as to what it may mean. You will begin to see how the Holy Spirit is using your dreams to bring you spiritual understanding.

7

How Your Dreams Can Help You Find Peace of Mind

Why are dreams so important? They are one way the ECK, or Holy Spirit, gives us Its guidance.

Nearly all his life, a man from Ghana has had a recurring dream to show him coming fortune. In the dream, he is always crossing a flooding river: The bigger the flooding, the greater his wealth. Recently, such a prophetic dream revealed that he would gain a large sum of money.

Soon after that he did, almost to the exact amount.

A woman from Washington State has universally prophetic dreams. Such dreams go beyond the personal life of the dreamer and take in world events.

In one of her dreams, she foresaw the volcanic explosion of Mount Saint Helens three years before it occurred in May 1980. In another, she witnessed the destructive earthquake in San Francisco a few years before it happened in October 1989. She does not pursue these dreams; they just come. They warn her to steer clear of the immediate areas of danger.

What do the above dreamers hold in common? Both are members of Eckankar. Both have studied the

ECK dream discourses, monthly lessons on the spiritual workings of dreams.

The ECK dream discourses tell you how to understand your dreams. People who appreciate the spiritual value of dreams study them to find peace of mind. That alone makes the ECK study of dreams every bit worthwhile.

Dreams are unique to the dreamer. Not everyone needs or wants prophetic dreams, so we'll look at other kinds—and their meanings—from members of Eckankar. Then I'll give a short technique to help you remember your own dreams, if you don't already.

A dream can also show a past life. In the following case, a young woman had read the first lesson of *The ECK Dream 2 Discourses*. In it, I said that some of today's younger ECKists had lived a past life as recently as World War II. This is her story:

In a dream, she learned of her death during the Japanese attack on Pearl Harbor.

As a young sailor then, she had realized she did not want power, glory, conquest, or anything related to all that. Death came when she ran up from below deck and entered the hatchway, where a stray bullet found her.

After her dream, she made plans to travel to Hawaii on vacation and visit the USS *Arizona* Memorial. When she and her husband arrived there, she began to tremble for no clear reason. She also developed a sudden, childish fear of losing her husband and Eckankar, both of which she held dear. What had caused her sense of loss?

In her life as a young sailor, she had had few regrets about leaving the war. Yet her early passing left her with the feeling of having missed out on something of unequaled spiritual value in that lifetime.

Had she once met Paul Twitchell, who became the Living ECK Master and founder of Eckankar in 1965? He had also been a U.S. sailor in the Pacific during the war.

Her untimely death in battle—as a man then—left her feeling that she'd lost a once-in-a-lifetime chance for spiritual growth. Her dream and later visit to Pearl Harbor helped her discover this unconscious fear. Now she can let go of the past and get on with her life.

The college student in the next story also had a dream that connected her physical and spiritual life. It all began with what looked like two strokes of luck.

Dreams had intrigued her since childhood. They were always vivid. When she related them to her friends and family, they would laugh and say, "You and your dreams." Her dreams were very real to her, but she could never understand the meaning they held.

One day she was in the college library, looking for a book to answer questions she hadn't yet put into words. She wandered aimlessly among the stacks, searching for a title to catch her eye. Then by chance she saw a book on Eckankar by Paul Twitchell. Though she had been to that area of the library many times before, she could not recall seeing that particular book. Quickly, she skimmed the first few pages, then literally skipped to class.

By chance again, an acquaintance gave her three more books on Eckankar. She had read a few chapters of one, when she had a dream with a white falcon. She was watching the bird with her fiancé. In the dream he was skeptical about her claim that the white falcon felt an attraction for her. To prove her point, she held up her right hand, and the falcon flew down to perch there.

In her mind, the falcon embodied wisdom. Whenever she voiced a question to which the answer was yes, it would fly toward her. When the answer was no, it would fly away.

Once during the dream she asked the white falcon a question about witchcraft. This time it remained on her hand, but bent down and pecked her finger. This was as if to say, Witchcraft can only bring you pain.

She remembered only a fragment of that dream upon awakening. Later in the day, upset by mounting problems, she was losing control. Then the white falcon flashed into her mind, and her tension eased considerably. The ECK, or Holy Spirit, had brought comfort to her on the wings of this white falcon.

Now she feels ready to start on the path of ECK. When she becomes a member of Eckankar, she can choose to receive *The ECK Dream 1 Discourses*. She will then learn of the many ways that the Holy Spirit gives wisdom and understanding through dreams.

Why does someone need the ECK teachings if he already has vivid dreams? Regular dreams do not come with the key to spiritual understanding. And what is that key? It is a little-known name for God, HU.

The word *HU* is an ancient name for God that has a unique ability to lift one into a higher state of awareness. The dream exercise that I promised you earlier centers around this special word. One way to open yourself to the wisdom of your dreams is to sing HU (pronounced *hue*). Sing it either softly or silently for a few minutes before bedtime. This sacred name for God will charge you spiritually. Then go to sleep as usual.

Now you have two necessary parts to spiritual understanding: your dreams and HU, the ancient name for God. Yet you need another item to complete this triad: a dream journal.

Whenever you have a dream, jot it down in a notebook. Right after describing the dream, write down your feelings as to what it may mean. Some keep a tape recorder by their bed. Others awaken at night and merely fix one or two points of their dream in mind and record it later.

If you put any time at all into this dream exercise, you will begin to see how the Holy Spirit is using your dreams to bring you spiritual understanding. The spiritual program of ECK dream study can help you find peace of mind.

What greater success or happiness could we hope to gain?

A large percentage of people claim at least one vision, a strong and unforgettable dream, or an out-of-
body experience.

8

How Karma and Reincarnation Lead to Spiritual Freedom

What benefit do the ECK teachings offer you over those of every other path to God? In the simplest terms, they offer spiritual freedom.

In a 1993 Doonesbury cartoon by Garry Trudeau, a young husband and wife go shopping for a church. They interview the young pastor of a very liberal church that has a mishmash of religion plus a touch of self-help programs. He calls it twelve-step Christianity. His ministry says each person is a recovering sinner. The meat of his offer to the couple is to help them overcome denial, find a spirit of recommitment, and gain redemption.

The couple balks. Doesn't redemption imply the word *guilt?* But the young pastor says he finds few occasions to use it, and then only to keep his flock from going astray. However, the couple feels there is already too much negativity in the world without having to add guilt to the equation. They'd like a church that's supportive, a place to feel good about themselves. Guilt does not fit the standard.

Unsure anymore of what to look for in a religion, the husband is ready to settle for a church that offers racquetball as a benefit. His wife talks him out of it.

Each religion holds out some promise to its followers. The word of Christianity to its people is the redemption of sins, a problem that stems from Adam and Eve, who disobeyed God in the Garden of Eden. Yet for their error, all future generations should carry the blame. A Christian, lost spiritually at birth, has the stigma of this original sin automatically fastened to him. Original sin means inborn guilt.

By contrast, the ECK teachings speak not of guilt but of responsibility. People are where they have put themselves. The theory of one lifetime per person is an example of an immature theology, for it does not account for the fact of reincarnation and karma. These two parts of the ECK teachings put the responsibility of a person's life directly where it belongs—upon the individual.

All people make their own world.

Where does spiritual freedom fit into the ECK teachings? God has placed each Soul upon earth to gain the spiritual purity and experience It needs to become a Co-worker with God. From the very beginning, many lifetimes ago, Soul made blunders. It was like an infant first having to find out how to crawl, then walk, while learning its place in the family and society.

Growth and development are a natural part of the divine order.

The ECK teachings say that people create karma, a debt with Divine Spirit, by ignorance of divine law. Time and experience will teach them better. However, it usually takes lifetimes to work off primary, daily, and reserve karma, because people forget their divine nature. This forgetfulness shows up in anger, vanity, greed, and other harmful traits. The result is more karma.

For that reason, we speak of the wheel of karma and reincarnation. More karma brings on more lifetimes. However fast people run, they must go even faster to stay ahead of their deeds, which threaten to catch and swallow them. Is there no end to this cycle?

There surely is. After an individual has passed so many lives in one religion or another, been whipped this way and that by life, it eventually dawns on him there is no way to beat the game alone. All running gets him is more running. At this point, a change occurs, perhaps as spiritual doubt. Or maybe it's a vision. A large percentage of people in the United States claim at least one vision, a strong and unforgettable dream, or an out-of-body experience. That experience is a wake-up call from the Mahanta, the Living ECK Master.

From that moment on, they become the seekers.

Yet they may spend the rest of this life in the church of their youth, too scared to leave it for a path like ECK, which gives them more satisfying answers. They are still the seekers. Perhaps in the next lifetime, they will find the courage to say, "What am I doing here? What is the meaning of life?"

Eckankar can show all people the most direct route home to God.

Yes, there is a quicker exit from the wheel of karma and reincarnation, but most people will settle for a longer, more difficult way home.

What about spiritual freedom? It is Soul's final release from the Law of Karma and Reincarnation. The ECK teachings say that to live a karmaless life, one must do everything in the name of God. At first, the Dream Master is the teacher. This teacher is the dream form of the Mahanta, the Living ECK Master. God has given him the spiritual power to act as both the Inner and Outer Master for those who want a more direct way out of these lower worlds. A guide and wayshower, he carries the key to the Light and Sound of God, two necessary parts of divine love.

Freedom from karma and reincarnation is spiritual freedom. This is the goal of everyone who has the spiritual maturity to see through the hollow promises of the immature religions.

Love is the force that returns Soul to God. For the path of truth starts in the heart, and the journey home to God begins with meeting the Mahanta in either a dream or in person. The Spiritual Exercises of ECK give strength and comfort, for these simple daily contemplations give one a stronger bond with the Divine Being. We call the path of ECK the Easy Way.

So the main benefit of ECK is spiritual freedom.

The entire aim of life is to find that freedom. Though the earth may shake and tremble, the person who loves God above all else will endure with peace of heart and mind.

A dream about failure usually means that using the same methods as in the past will continue to lead to failure. But if a dreamer can break old habits and try something new to solve problems, it's a new ball game.

9

The Purpose of Dreams

The works of ECK give a balance between the inner and outer teachings. Here is a story from the inner planes. It illustrates the power of dreaming big and working hard, two keys to success in any world.

One night, on the inner planes, I went to a local college football game. As usual, the home team lost. And in accord with its dismal win-loss record, the team turned in a completely uninspired effort. So the locker room was a gloomy place after the game, even though it was full of people—the many friends and family of the coach and players.

The coach was a strict disciplinarian. He got on well with his players, but they could not win for him. The coach and I had little in common. So I mostly avoided him, because we lived and worked in two different worlds.

This evening was to be different, though. The crowd was still thick at a refreshment table inside the locker room when he called me over.

"I had a dream," he said. "Could you tell me its meaning?"

A dream interpreter must always allow for the

51

chance that his interpretation might be wrong, so he leaves an opening for the dreamer should the news look bad.

The coach briefly told his dream. For the second time within a few days, he had heard an orchestra play an enchanting piece of music. The musicians did not finish the song either time. Yet the music was of such haunting beauty that he wanted nothing more than to hear its conclusion.

Unknown to him, the heavenly music was exactly that: the Music of God. It comes from Divine Spirit, the Voice of God. Its purpose is to call Souls that are ready and show them the way home to Sugmad— another name for God, or the Ocean of Love and Mercy. As the ECK texts put it: Soul has heard and is yearning to go.

But from all appearances, this coach did not work on a very high spiritual level, so he would not have understood an interpretation that spoke of this Music of God.

Yet a dream interpreter has a duty to speak the truth. That is not to say that he must be unkind, because it is a kind spirit who leaves an open door for a dreamer in case the analysis is wrong.

Before I could say anything, he spoke. "I think my two dreams are trying to say that I've reached the end of my career in this lifetime."

Unfortunately, that was my first impression too.

"I'll never get to coach at the state level," he added, looking closely at me for confirmation.

Then the ECK let me see the options of possibility.

"Dreams aren't final," I said. "I can't tell the times a dream appeared to point out failure to me, but I refused to accept the verdict. A dream about failure usually means that using the same methods as in the past will continue to lead to failure. But if a dreamer can break old habits and try something new to solve problems, it's a new ball game."

The coach was catching on.

"You mean my career's not over?" he stated, half in reply and half in question.

"There is a lot of power in the human spirit," I replied. "If you could unlock the spirit of your team, you'd see miracles. There is a power in people who dream big and who try hard."

Then two young players from the team returned to the locker room, which had cleared of most people during our conversation. They drew the coach aside to ask a favor. Immediately, he went to a metal toolbox and began digging around inside it. I mistook the action. I assumed that he had plans of game strategy in the box that he could not wait to show his two star players. They just happened to return to the locker room during the height of his excitement.

In fact, the situation was very different. Their car had a flat tire, and they were late for a postgame school dance. So the coach was not trying to dig out and explain next week's strategy.

I called to him on my way out. "By the way," I said, "something else always helps. That's to listen to the ideas of others when all yours hit the wall."

With a quick thumbs-up sign, he shouted back, "You mean, let *them* mount the tire!" His excitement was no longer about his own dreams of aspiration. He had put them aside to help his young players fix the tire and get to the party before it was over. He remembered his youth.

I knew that he now had the right idea about winning. Go for success in life, but not at the expense of other people's dreams. Help them meet their dreams, and they will help you meet yours.

Another student walked with me to my residence some three or four blocks away. The sidewalk ran up some small hills and down again, like a rising and falling wave of the ocean.

"As we get older," I said to him, "these little hills become like mountains. Even though it requires more effort to accomplish our dreams, we must always follow them."

That is the purpose of dreams.

When her spiritual guide, the Mahanta, wanted to remind her to avoid gossip and honor the Law of Silence, she had a dream in which something unpleasant was in her mouth.

10

Dreams, Your Road to Heaven

Our dreams are the forgotten road to heaven. This was once a nearly absolute truth. That is, until the teachings of ECK surfaced in 1965 to encourage people to look for the lost doorway between heaven and earth: their dreams.

Dreams are the starting point for many who wish to begin the spiritual journey to God and do it in the easiest possible way. There simply is no better way to start than with our dreams. Good works may carry us far along this holy journey, and prayer is indeed a boon, but generally we can learn more about the true nature of God through the secret knowledge of dreams.

Daydreams, night dreams, contemplation, Soul Travel—all are steps in the pursuit of heaven. In Eckankar, the student is under the protection of a spiritual guide known as the Mahanta. This is the Spiritual Traveler. As the Mahanta, he is the Inner Master, the one who comes on the inner planes to impart knowledge, truth, and wisdom. But he also has an outer side. Here he is known as the Living ECK Master. Thus, the spiritual leader of Eckankar can work both inwardly and outwardly with all who come to learn of God and life.

Those who want his spiritual direction may choose to become members of Eckankar. As part of their first year of study, they may receive *The ECK Dream 1 Discourses.*

Each month, the individual is sent a six-page discourse that explores the spiritual world of dreams. This study is different from any other study he may have made in the past, for it deals entirely with Soul. What is Soul's responsibility to God and all living things? Key to this dream knowledge is divine love: where and how do you find it?

A person who travels in his dream worlds is assured of the Mahanta's protection, because heaven is a place of many dimensions. To learn about them, read Paul Twitchell's *The Tiger's Fang.*

In those lower heavens that lie between earth and the true worlds of God, there are shady people who like nothing better than to cheat or harm innocent victims. In Africa, for instance, the power of black magic is very strong. An African man reported a dream in which a group of men and women took him to a high place. Unknown to him, these people were warlocks and witches. When they reached the top of this place, which was a towering seawall, a woman in the group told him to jump into the sea. But he knew that all who jumped from that height never came back.

"Jump!" she urged. As if hypnotized, he began to move toward the edge of the wall. At that moment, the Mahanta appeared. The group vanished. The Master smiled and patted the dreamer on his shoulder; then the dreamer awoke.

What few would recognize is that the Mahanta prevented the dreamer's death. It often happens that a dreamer, who does not have the protection of the

Mahanta, simply dies in his sleep. The doctor writes off the cause as heart failure or some other physical condition. Often as not, however, the dreamer had wandered beyond the safe limits of his inner world and met a psychic criminal, who was responsible for his death. An experience that did not have to be, had he known of the Mahanta, the Living ECK Master.

Dreams are one road to heaven. Another way to enter is through contemplation: a few minutes each day of spiritual relaxation in which the individual sits with his eyes closed and sings the holy name of God. This word is HU. The Master comes, in time, to take him into the worlds of heaven, the Far Country. With the Master along, what may otherwise have been a nightmare turns out to have a spiritual end.

In the following instance, the Mahanta was the guide for an ECK initiate during an experience in contemplation. The Master took her to a large white-domed temple with stately pillars. In front of the temple was an enormous Buddha made of iron—the temple's guardian. He was seated on a circular platform.

"Bow down and worship me!" he commanded.

Awed by this thirty-foot-tall entity, she immediately began to prostrate herself before him. But the Master said, "We don't worship this entity." To the Buddha, he said, "I just want to show her something of interest down the left corridor." The Buddha blinked his massive eyes once, very slowly, in approval. The way was clear for them to enter the temple and for her to learn the secret wisdom of ECK which was stored there.

More often, though, we start our study of heaven through dreams. They are a most natural way. The student of ECK finds that his dreams become ever more spiritual as he continues his search for God.

The mind, however, is the chief obstacle in the search for God. It tries to have the dreamer forget dreams in which the Mahanta imparts divine wisdom. So the Master must bypass this wall created by the mind.

One way the Mahanta, the Living ECK Master accomplishes this is seen in a dream study by an ECKist. When the Mahanta wanted to remind her to avoid gossip and honor the Law of Silence, she had a dream in which something unpleasant was in her mouth. When the Master's lesson was on the "play" of life, her dream experiences dealt with school, group meetings, clubs, dorms, households, even pageants. When it was necessary for her to recall travel through higher levels of consciousness, her dreams were of stairs, steps, elevators, mazes of rooms, and even of herself on a child's swing.

Dreams are a road to heaven. They are not the only road; they do not go straight to the highest heaven, but they do offer a sound beginning for anyone who sincerely wants to find God.

In ECK, we are familiar with dreams of past lives. Other dreams give us insight into our health, family concerns, love interests, business plans, and guidance in how to live our lives with minute-to-minute care, if we are interested in developing our study of dreams to such a degree. But the most important dream category is the spiritual dream. It tells us something about our present life, with all its struggles. We learn about hidden motives, which most people wish to leave undisturbed in the dark corners of their minds.

Here is a spiritual dream, so that when you have one you will have a measure to compare it with. A dreamer awoke in her dream to find herself alongside the ocean. A high mound of sand ran parallel to the water, like a breakwater. She noticed she was on the side nearest the ocean. Looking closely at the mound of sand, she found little booklets buried in it and picked one up. An ECK Master came and read the message in the booklet for her.

"You've won a white used car," he said.

Used? She pulled another booklet from the mound, hoping for a message that said she had won a new white car. Instead, the ECK Master read: "You've won $113,000 in groceries." A second before she awoke, she found herself on the other side of the mound, away from the ocean.

The spiritual meaning came to her loud and clear: She had taken a step backward in her spiritual life. It came as a shock to her to see how attached she had become to worldly things. Only a month earlier she had written a two-word letter to the Living ECK Master: "I'm ready." She meant, for a higher state of consciousness.

This dream was a humbling experience. She now realized that the Mahanta had given her the used car in the dream because it was right for her at the time. It was the Master's gift, no matter how "used" it may have seemed to her. She was able to take a new look at herself, honestly. From that dream she was then able to move up spiritually as she had desired.

Many more stories could be told about dreamers who have been enriched by their dreams. The study of dreams is an art, a highly interesting spiritual endeavor. It gives deep satisfaction to all who wish to learn more about themselves through personal experience.

Above all, dreams are of priceless spiritual worth to us, because they open our personal road to heaven.

Your dreams are like a telescope that can give a better view of something that is normally out of your reach: your spiritual side. That includes how you act, feel, reflect, think, react, and even love.

11

Tips on How to Interpret Your Dreams

Dreams. Dreams, the stuff of wonder, fear, the unknown — but they are always certain to pique our curiosity.

Dreams. They were the reason for the good fortune of Joseph of the Old Testament. He overcame all odds — treachery by his brothers, slavery, and imprisonment — to rise in stature and power until he was second only to the mighty pharaoh of Egypt.

Dreams hold an aura of mystery. They give power to anyone who can — or claims to — interpret them. Elias Howe, inventor of the sewing machine, tried for years to develop his invention, but without success. Until, in a dream, he got orders to finish it or pay with his life. Strong motivation, indeed.

Among the many examples of the influence of dreams, there is the one of Samuel Clemens, the American humorist known as Mark Twain. He foresaw the death of his brother Henry, who also worked on the riverboats of the Mississippi River during the 1850s. One night, Twain awoke from a nightmare in which he saw the metal coffin of his brother. On it lay a bouquet of white flowers, a red rose in the middle.

A few weeks later, his brother suffered severe injuries from a boiler explosion on the river. He died shortly after.

Upon his arrival a few days later, Twain found the setting exactly as it had appeared in his dream. Some people had taken pity upon his brother and had collected money to buy an expensive metal coffin, instead of the wooden boxes usually used for river accidents. As Twain paid his last respects, a woman entered the room and placed on the coffin a bouquet of white flowers with a single red rose in the middle.

Dreams touch every level of our life. They may let us glimpse the future, or give suggestions for healing, or share insights into our relationships. Above all, they can and will steer us more directly toward God.

What is this fantasy about dreams?

First, understand that the dream world is anything but a fantasy. A "confused" dream simply shows the inability of our mind to accept truth head-on, so it bends the facts and artfully weaves them into a story line that is less likely to cause us distress. Yes, dreams are real.

A mother listening to her young daughter tell of an inner experience from the night before dismissed it offhand as only a dream. The girl quickly corrected her. "Not just a dream, Mom," she said. "It was real."

So, first, understand that the land of dreams is an actual place. Second, any experience you gain in the dream world is as useful to you spiritually as any of those you may have here in the human body.

To grasp the universal nature of dreams, take a step back and imagine that you are standing at the top of all worlds. The identity that can do that, to command a view even of creation itself, is the real you—eternal Soul. Soul is a child of God, and, by nature, godlike. And so It can share in the divine attributes of wisdom, joy, freedom, and divine love. So why doesn't It? Why don't you?

Your dreams are like a telescope that can give a better view of something that is normally out of reach: your spiritual side. That includes how you act, feel, reflect, think, react, and even love. Most people fear putting the telescope of dreams to their eye, afraid of what they might see.

So what about interpreting dreams? Where do the beginners start? Do they begin in the bookstore, buying volumes of books that supposedly give the inside scoop on dreams?

No. That's not to say they won't learn something by reading books on dreams, because they will. They will learn the many ways that people approach the dream world: through symbols, the emotions, as outer causes, or as riddles. These only give a small part of the picture. If people have the wisdom and insight, and spend enough time at it, they can eventually piece all the odd ends together and come up with their own dream patchwork of sorts.

Yet it will still miss the beauty and wonder of *living,* in full consciousness, in your heavens of dreams.

Dreams have a meaning at every step—the human, emotional, causal, mental, subconscious, and spiritual levels. They correspond to the six planes of existence, spoken of so often in the ECK works—the Physical, Astral, Causal, Mental, Etheric, and Soul planes. And each deals with a part of us. Each of our dreams comes mainly from one of these areas.

Our task is to keep the interpretation of dreams simple.

Look at each dream on one of three levels. They are about our daily life, our emotions and thoughts, and, less often, about the pure spiritual side. So, simply put, there are dreams about our everyday events, our emotional well-being, and our relationship with God.

The beauty of dreams is that they go with you everywhere, no matter what. They are a portable treasure. You need only recall them, to recognize them as a divine gift to gain insight into your true spiritual nature. Never are you without your dreams.

Is it possible to go somewhere for the weekend and say, "Oh, I forgot to pack my dreams"?

No, they are always with you, because they are a part of you and you of them. They give a broader picture of yourself and the great spiritual potential that lies within you.

I would say that some figures of state, church, and science understate the value of dreams, for they often ridicule or punish those who speak too freely about the dream life. A dreamer is often an independent being. He looks inwardly, instead of outwardly, for the real answers to life.

My plan was to give a sample of dreams and explain them, but there are already many such examples in the ECK dream discourses. This is a chance to speak directly to your heart, to you as Soul.

Here, then, are a few thoughts on how to enter a better spiritual life through the doorway of dreams:

1. Dream—get plenty of rest for a few days. Then go to sleep with the intention of remembering some of the places you visit while your human self lies sleeping. (It helps to write the dreams down as soon as you awaken.)

2. Interpret your dreams—ask the Dream Master (my inner self) to let you see each dream on three

levels: the daily, the emotional/mental, and the spiritual.

3. Realize your dreams—take the dream lessons and apply them to your everyday life.

You can make this study of dreams as easy as you like. However, you need to give the ECK Dream Master permission to help you understand them.

Your consent can be as simple as saying, "Please, Harold, help me remember my dreams and understand them."

It's that easy.

If you want your dreams to lift you into a higher state of awareness and joy, you have only to ask. My task is to help you become mindful of yourself in the real worlds, the dreamlands of God.

I'll see you in your dreams.

Seeing a past life means it has a spiritual lesson for you right now.

12

The Answer Man Can

The ECK teachings set a high standard for getting knowledge, truth, and wisdom. Yet, despite all the new areas they open for you in your spiritual quest to become a better person, they also raise more questions.

Some time ago, ECK youth asked me the following questions. So the Answer Man will try to answer them. The title for this could as well be "The Answer Man Can—Sometimes," because a given response may not work for everyone. In fact, you can almost say it won't.

Truth, like each of you, is a unique expression of the divine will that made you. That means you will understand the answer when you have the right sort of spiritual experience behind you. Don't worry, it will come.

So here goes. These questions are all about dreams.

• *What is the purpose of bad dreams?* No purpose, really. However, they do show that you are in deep water and you can't swim. They reveal a fear or a weakness. The purpose of a bad dream is not necessarily to point out your vulnerability, but you certainly become aware of it.

A bad dream may be one of several things. It may be a past-life recall. As such, it simply lets you see a challenge from the distant past. How did you handle it?

Usually, the dreamer awakens before finding out. So then he can take the experience into contemplation and ask the Dream Master to give him some clues as to its meaning.

A bad dream, by its shocking nature, is instructional about some spiritual point that the dreamer has overlooked in his waking life.

• *Why, when I'm falling in my sleep, do I land on my back?* A cat, you know, generally lands on its feet. A cat is alert. It instinctively flips itself upright as a matter of survival.

Your dreams are telling you to examine your life carefully. In some way, you are not as aware as you could be, in a very important matter. For example, have you studied enough for finals? Is your checking account in order? Are you showing love and kindness to your dear ones?

A dream of falling on your back is the Dream Master's way of telling you something very important. Look again. Look at yourself again.

• *Why can you remember past lives, and how can they help you?* A saying in the markets is this: "Learn from the mistakes of other traders—you can never make them all yourself."

From a spiritual viewpoint, though, you can. Fortunately, most of your karma came from unconscious deeds in a past life, so there's no need to repeat them.

A dreamer who can tap into the Time Track through his dreams has a spiritual shortcut at his command. The Dream Master calls up a past life for the benefit

70

of the ECKist. Seeing a past life means it has a spiritual lesson for you right now. Perhaps the Master saw you were about to repeat a mistake you made before. So, in this case, a past-life dream is a warning. It means, "Look again!"

• *Can you have a dream without seeing anything?* For sure. However, you will *hear* something. Remember the two aspects of the ECK (Holy Spirit)? Right, the Light and Sound. A dream is one way—of many—that Divine Spirit talks to people, although with symbols. Usually, a dream is a visual experience.

But there is the other sort. In a dream of the second kind, the dreamer finds himself in a void without any light at all.

He does hear sounds, though. Sometimes, there may be the sound of rushing wind similar to that of a jet tearing through the air. Or again it may be a sound of nature: thunder in the distance, rainfall, a birdsong, or the like.

Again, it could be an inner communication. This can take the form of telepathy: a voice more real and dynamic than any human voice. It gives the dreamer some vital spiritual instruction.

All sound, no light.

• *Why, when you run in your dream, does it feel like you can't move?* This special dream is a Soul Travel technique. The Dream Master uses it to help the dreamer develop the spiritual strength to explore his own inner worlds in full consciousness.

Sometimes it feels like trying to run in a deep swimming pool. The dreamer exerts himself to the fullest, trying to run. But this dream is only a mockup, or a springboard. If he succeeds in breaking through the water's resistance, he often finds himself in another setting. Often, a person awakens in the Soul body. He can now look at his human body asleep on the bed.

This out-of-body experience doesn't come to all dreamers, only to those who need it. Need it for what? For proof of the immortal state of Soul.

Once the dreamer sees what the Soul body is like, the Dream Master returns him to his sleeping body. A second later, the individual is rubbing the sleep from his eyes, thinking about the glorious and natural state of freedom he just experienced.

Then it finally hits him. "Hey! That was Soul Travel."

• *Do all dreams mean something?* Yes, they do. But that doesn't mean the human mind has the capacity to understand all the spiritual experiences that we have.

The human mind, for all its power, is a very limited instrument in comparison to Soul. But don't worry. If the meaning of a certain dream is important for you spiritually, the Dream Master will send the message again and again through other dreams until you do get its meaning.

So relax and enjoy the ride.

* * *

These questions were all good ones. Yet they only begin to touch on the mystery and elegance of you, the dreamer. The teachings of ECK delve much deeper into the nature of truth as it touches you spiritually.

Your dreams are a good beginning.

What is true worship? It is any act that brings one closer to God. The answer is to do everything with love for God. Such acts need no praise.

13

What Is True Worship?

You can't pull the wool over God's eyes. When the leaders of two opposing nations call upon God to help them in their combat against each other, each believes he has the ear of the true Deity—his own God. Yet, it is the same God over all.

When the coaches of two sports teams are ready to lock in battle and pray for aid, each feels that the one, true Deity will show him special favor. Of course, when the game ends, there is only one victor. Is God a sports fan? Did God have money on the winners, or did He have some other special interest in them?

It has always struck me odd to hear about such frivolous prayers. What makes anyone think that God supports war, sports, or a certain religion, for example? Does God really get down into the noise level of our games?

Have you ever noticed that when a team prays to God for victory and wins, nobody gives Him credit after the game. When the TV cameras zero in on the stars of the game, how often do they say, "We won by the grace of God!" And when someone does bring the name of God into it after the game, it's almost a sign of boorishness.

And who has ever heard the losing coach blame God after a loss?

We, the human race, are a funny lot. If God cared about the warts of the human race, He would have his TV tuned to its pratfalls and silly comments—typically done in His name.

Prayer is sometimes a part of worship. What is true worship? To my mind, it is any act that brings one closer to God.

And true prayer? It is either a private or public act that acknowledges the wisdom and all-seeing power of God. Also, it is having the grace to accept God's will as it appears, though it may differ from our own idea of what His will should be.

So, true prayer does not try to bend the will of God to suit our own purposes.

Why pray for wealth when God has seen fit to give us poverty? Certainly, the Deity's vision is better than our own, in that His wish is for our spiritual, not material, gain. And how does this show up? In our struggle to survive, or move out of our poverty, it is spiritually that we gain the most.

ECKists are now ready to move into the world and be channels for ECK, the Holy Spirit. Of course, many have already done that. Now, however, with the Temple of ECK as the center post of the missionary effort in ECK, we must look closely at our own idea of what true worship is. When giving service to others in the name of Sugmad, is it really necessary to tell them we have another name for God? How can our charity stand on its own? For those who want to know, the answer is to do everything with love for God. Such acts need no praise.

How can you tell when someone—even you—is living a life of true worship? Simply look to see how much charity that person demonstrates toward others in his or her daily life.

What is charity? It is our expression of goodwill toward others.

In whatever of a thousand or more forms it may take, our behavior speaks volumes about whether or not we have charity. One who loves God will serve others. Of the countless ways to give that service, the way of another may not be our own. In whatever way we choose to pass along to others the blessings of the Holy Spirit upon us, we should need no praise from another in doing it. We serve others because we love God. If there is any other reason behind our so-called acts of charity, they are not true charity.

What is the connection between true worship, prayer, and charity? If our relationship with God is one of love, we will act with charity toward others. Our prayers will accept our lot as God has given it, depending upon better conditions to come from our own efforts. True prayer does not put off on God the responsibility that we must take for our own lives.

Let's look at an example of charity:

An ECKist helps at a crisis center in Portland, Oregon. Late one winter's day, he received a call from a woman in her fifties whose landlord had just evicted her from her apartment. Could he help her find a place to stay that night?

All the shelters in Portland were full already, but he knew of one in Vancouver, Washington—just across the Columbia river—that might have an opening. However, the line was busy.

With each failure for the call to go through, the homeless woman became more upset. Finally, she said, "Would you pray for me?" He agreed. Then she added: "Please begin with 'Dear Jesus.'" He wondered how he, an ECKist, could join prayers with a Christian woman. But he did as she asked, putting as much ECK into the prayer as possible. After the many unsuccessful tries, his next call went through.

"Thank you so much!" she cried. To her mind, it was the prayer to Jesus that had gotten her a place to stay that night.

What actually happened here? Perhaps the earlier calls had not gotten through to the shelter because the ECKist and the woman in need were pushing too hard to tell God what to do. The prayer worked for this reason: They finally each surrendered their will to God's. That is when a prayer is true.

The ECKist, reviewing the experience later, saw that what really mattered in this situation was that one Soul was helping another. It made no difference how they reached surrender to God's will: through contemplation or prayer. Nor was the religion of any importance—Eckankar or Christianity.

What, then, is true worship?

True worship is *listening* to God. It is not talking the ears off God. It is not demanding that God do something this way or that—usually *our* way. Listening to God is an often forgotten form of prayer.

Remember this when you do the Spiritual Exercises of ECK.

You have been in nearly every possible religion, both existing and spent. How did each prepare you for the path of Eckankar, which offers the most direct teachings of the Light and Sound of God?

14

A Quick Look
at World Religions

In 1965, Eckankar made its appearance as a new spiritual teaching among the religions of earth. It is the keystone of all religions. You have been in nearly every possible religion, both existing and spent.

Let's review some of the major religions from your present or past lives. In order of size, these are Christianity, Islam, Hinduism, Buddhism, and Judaism. Try to imagine what attracted you to them. How did each prepare you for the path of ECK today?

* * *

• Christianity, largest of all religions, claims 33 percent of the world's population. Although it has split into many divisions and sects, we may safely say that it is about Jesus, who became the Christ. God in human form, he was willing to suffer and die for the sins of mankind. That was a sweeping idea to the ancient world. Christians may differ in their views about the nature of Christ (how much God and how much man), but most consider him to be the way to salvation.

Christianity speaks of the Holy Spirit, but has erred in trying to reduce It to a person. The Holy Spirit is not a person at all, but the Voice of God. We know It as the Sound and Light of God, or ECK.

• Islam, the second largest religion, has only about half as many members as Christianity. That, however, is more than 17 percent of the world's population. Its major belief is that one must submit completely to the will of God. Hence the word *Islam,* which means "submission." The one God is Allah. A Muslim's duty is to give his life over in complete obedience to Allah. Each person enjoys free will and must account for his deeds on Judgment Day. A person who obeys God's law in this life finds the rewards of paradise in the next.

Sufis, the mystics of Islam, have long known the elements of the Light and Sound of God. But they have yet to learn of the Mahanta, the Living ECK Master. He can guide them to the high states of heaven beyond the Soul Plane and help them realize God.

• Hinduism is third in size among religions and boasts 13 percent of the world's population. A collection of many beliefs and practices, it teaches man's separation from the Supreme Deity. In that, man has also lost his own powers of creation. Through yoga, however, he can find his divine nature and so end the cycle of birth and rebirth and its burden of karma. Thus he finds spiritual freedom through union with God.

In Eckankar, we do not seek to become one with God—which is outside the bounds of possibility—but one with ECK.

Hinduism itself has nothing directly related to the Sound Current as Eckankar knows It. However, Kabir, a Muslim by birth, introduced basic ECK teachings in his poems, which he hoped would unite the Muslims and Hindus. Kabir attracted a band of followers, among whom was Nanak. Expanding upon Kabir's teachings,

Guru Nanak became the founder of the Sikh religion, which did carry elements of the Light and Sound to India.

• Buddhism comes in a distant fourth in size of world religions. Yet, Buddhists make up some 6 percent of the world's population.

This religion, an offshoot of Hinduism, began in the sixth century B.C. with Siddhartha Gautama. After steadfast meditation under a fig tree at Bodh Gaya, he reached what he felt was supreme enlightenment. It was actually cosmic consciousness, which comes on the Mental Plane. Still, it was a high state for those times and one which few reach even now. After that, he was the Buddha, or the Awakened One. He spent his life teaching that the potential for Buddhahood lies asleep in all and needs only to awaken.

The Four Noble Truths of Buddha say: (1) Life is suffering; (2) desire is the cause of it. (3) The way to overcome suffering is through nirvana, the state of no desires. (4) The middle path to nirvana is along the Eightfold Noble Path. These eight practices bring freedom from the Wheel of Life (karma and rebirth).

Critics debate whether Buddhism is truly a religion, because Buddha never spoke about God, only nirvana. There is nothing in Buddhism about the Sound and Light of God. Its purpose was to provide a common grounding in moral teaching for the caste-split society of India.

• Judaism is much smaller than other mainline religions, but its impact in the world outstrips its size. Further, it is a parent to both Christianity and Islam. Yet, Jews make up but three-tenths of 1 percent of the world's population.

It was the first religion with the belief in one God (Yahweh). Absolute creator and ruler of the universe,

Yahweh gave love to all. However, He set up a special covenant with the Jews, the Chosen People. This requires them to bring the message of Yahweh to others through the example of their daily lives.

In Judaism, the doctrine of salvation centers upon the hope that God will one day send a Messiah. He will redeem the Jews and set up His kingdom on earth. To speed the coming of God's kingdom, Jews can lead pious and ethical lives to testify to the holiness of creation.

The Light and Sound of God do appear in the Torah, the Jewish scriptures, but the Jews overlook the importance of them.

• Eckankar is among the new religions, which make up a little more than 2 percent of the world's population. However, this group is growing in both size and importance.

The teachings of ECK define the nature of Soul more carefully than do other current religions. Each person is Soul, a particle of God sent into the lower worlds (including earth) to gain spiritual experience. Purified by the spiritual exercises, he comes into contact with the Holy Spirit. His goal is spiritual freedom in this lifetime, after which he becomes a Co-worker with God, both here and in the next world. Karma and reincarnation are primary beliefs.

Key to the ECK teachings is the Mahanta, the Living ECK Master. He has the special ability to act as both Inner and Outer Master for ECK students. He is the prophet of Eckankar, given respect but not worship. He teaches the sacred name of God, HU, which lifts one spiritually into the Light and Sound of God, the ECK.

The ECK (the Holy Spirit) purifies one of karma (sin), making it possible for him to accept the full love of God in this lifetime. Then he gains wisdom, charity, and freedom.

Personal experience with the Light and Sound of God is the cornerstone of Eckankar. Of all the religions on earth today, Eckankar offers the most direct teachings of the Light and Sound of God. These twin pillars are missing in whole or in part from the rest. People who truly find these two aspects of God undergo a complete spiritual change. Life becomes fresh and new again, as it was in early childhood.

* * *

So how long have you been in ECK: twenty-five years or twenty-five centuries? In looking at these other religions, you can see that each lets its followers unfold in a certain direction.

And what can Eckankar offer you beyond the features of these other religions? It can prepare you to receive the Light and Sound of God. They alone can open you to the peace and divine love within you.

Gazing into the pool of Truth during a spiritual exercise, she saw her own reflection. It meant that she had only to look inside herself for the truth of God. That is a big turning point.

15

Turning Points

So very often the ECK, the Holy Spirit, furnishes new turning points in your life.

A turning point is life's way of giving you a chance to move ahead spiritually, though you must reach for the gift yourself. The path of ECK is all about the gift of turning points. The breath and love of God empower it, a path to help all who would reach the Kingdom of God in this lifetime.

Dolores loves the ECK, finding it easy to keep her attention on God and the goal of spiritual freedom.

One day as she was busy around the house, the doorbell rang—unusual, because it seldom worked. She ran, tripped, and stumbled her way to the door. Outside stood two young women with Bibles.

"We came to read the Bible to you," one said.

Dolores started to shut the door. But as she did, her temper began to flare: What right did these two Bible readers have intruding upon her privacy? Then her self-control snapped. She slammed the door so hard it actually shook the house.

Ashamed of her behavior, she began to wonder whether the Master would have been so rude as to slam the door on the two young missionaries. What had they done to her?

That experience was a turning point for Dolores, for it gave her a new insight into herself. *She* was the problem. The women had come to her door as visitors, with only good in mind, but the problem was in her reaction to them. What reason could excuse such behavior? After the incident, Dolores began to realize that she had hurt the feelings of the young women, who were only trying to make their way to spiritual freedom too.

To get spiritual freedom, one must first give it.

Since that day, she is polite to people of other faiths who unexpectedly appear at her home or call on the telephone. She now speaks with more love and kindness.

"Well, thank you for thinking of me, but I'm really not interested."

She is gentler with others. And each time she gives love and respect to people of other beliefs, it becomes even easier in the next situation. Where she used to show impatience and anger, she now gives love, because she remembers what it was like when she was on the same rung of the spiritual ladder.

Stacie, an ECK initiate, had already come to a turning point in understanding a while ago. Now she lets others have the same chance. If people need spiritual help, she gives them the tape *HU: A Love Song to God,* and her only reward is to watch the light go on inside them.

At her place of work is an Hispanic woman, a Catholic. The woman's estranged husband used to abuse her, but now that he is dying of leukemia and other complications, she has taken him back.

Stacie had a nudge to ask how he felt being so near to death. Before Eckankar, Stacie had also been a

Catholic, which gave her a sense of the couple's feelings. The woman told of his fear. So Stacie mentioned the HU tape to her and how anyone—regardless of faith—could get spiritual help by singing HU.

The woman asked her to bring the HU tape to work.

A few days later, when the woman had returned to work after a few days off, she asked Stacie where she could get a tape of her own. She'd seen a change in her husband. To her surprise, he listened to the tape and could now sleep better than in a long while.

You can find the path to love, wisdom, and spiritual freedom by singing HU every day, until HU becomes a part of you and you of it. Then go on to other Spiritual Exercises of ECK. They are in many of the books and discourses of ECK and will help you find your own turning points.

Leslie learned this herself. As she had begun a spiritual exercise, the word *pool* came up on the screen of her mind. The Mahanta then appeared to her. He asked, "How would you like to visit the Pool of ECK?"

In less than a second, they were in some other world.

The Pool of ECK was actually more like a small, glistening lake. "It is also the Pool of Truth," he said. "When one gazes into it, what reflects is truth. Ask any question. Then look into the pool and you will see truth."

So she asked, "What is the truth of God?"

Gazing into the mirrored surface of the water, she saw her own reflection, clear and pure. It meant that she had only to look inside herself for the truth of God, for it has existed within her from the beginning.

Then she asked, "What is the truth of the Temple of ECK?"

Looking into the pool again, she saw many ECK temples scattered around the world, with many people going to them. She understood this: The outer Temple is necessary to help people find their own inner truth, because the Temple of ECK and what it represents will open the spiritual eyes of people.

Again she asked, "What is the truth about the spiritual exercises?"

A thought struck her. At that very moment, she was in a special place—beside the Pool of Truth, a privilege that stemmed from doing the spiritual exercises. Then, walking into the Pool of Truth, she realized that because she did the Spiritual Exercises of ECK, she was opening herself to more truth. In time, she would become the living truth herself.

That is a big turning point.

So do the spiritual exercises, for they are a golden pathway to your own turning points on the road to God. They offer you God Consciousness, the chance of a lifetime.

Use what you are. This is another way of saying: Look for the windfall at your feet. Unless you learn to see the small blessings of God, you won't see the rest.

16

Use What You Are

Before the flight to the 1992 ECK European Seminar in Paris, I bought a novel to help pass the time. It was by a favorite author of mine, someone to trust on a long journey.

The book came from the airport bookstore, where I bought it a short while before departure. Very carefully, I stowed it in my suitcase, in the usual place for my reading material, where it would be easy to reach during the flight. It surprised me how easily it slid into the suitcase among the other books. I couldn't wait to get aboard, settle into my seat, and begin enjoying the story.

So after takeoff, I unzipped the travel bag and reached for the novel. It wasn't there. Anywhere. So I lugged the bag onto my lap, while Joan helped me check all three compartments. The book had simply vanished.

That changed my plans on the spot. So I pulled out other books, more in line with the new area of spiritual development.

Again, I had felt the hand of ECK, the Holy Spirit, and Its guidance. It had earlier given me a new spiritual course to follow, which I now learned meant giving up even some old reading matter. The ECK touches every corner.

Use what you are.

This is another way of saying: Look for the windfall at your feet. Unless you learn to see the small blessings of God, you won't see the rest.

On the same flight, I noticed a pattern from the person in the seat in front of me that wears on my patience. That person usually—not always, but usually—drops the seat back all the way. This time the seat's occupant was an elderly woman. Even before the plane began to taxi out to the runway, she reclined her seat into my face. There was a touch of grace, however. Most of the people throw it back suddenly, but she put it back ever so gently.

"See?" I told my wife. "Look around. Is anyone else reclining their seat yet?" Of course, only the seat ahead of me was back. A flight attendant came along eventually and had the woman put her seat up for takeoff.

The intervention was all too brief. A minute after the wheels were up, the seat eased back into my face again, likely for the entire seven-hour flight. The seating space on this airliner was tight, like sitting in a fruit box. Anyway, with this passenger's seat fully reclined, she then leaned forward, perched on the front edge of her seat, to visit with her seat companion. She sat like that well into the flight.

Outside, day quickly turned to night as the plane sped eastward. I was stiff in the cramped seat, still trying to read and study. Finally, resigning myself to a long flight with no reprieve, I shut my eyes. My good friend Peddar Zaskq, my former teacher and guide, appeared to me on the inner planes.

"Can you imagine?" I said. "Some people have no

grace or sense of others in their surroundings at all."

"Don't worry about it," he replied. "Try to catch some winks. I'll take care of it." So he left, and I fell into a light sleep.

A short while later, a commotion in the aisle awoke me. A flight attendant was in an earnest conversation with the woman in the forward seat. The woman had taken ill. After a few minutes of questioning, the crew member said it was probably only motion sickness, as the aircraft had flown into some turbulence. But would the woman like to sit in first class?

A minute later, the seat was vacant.

Use what you are.

Look around yourself for help in everyday life, because an answer will come as surely as a flower in spring to an alpine meadow.

Use What You Are is the title of a small book by Fun-Chang from East-West Publications. The author, who lived hundreds of years before the Christian era, tells the fable of a Chinese emperor. This emperor kept a close watch upon his subjects from the palace windows. Yet, as closely as he watched from afar, he remained aloof from the life of his subjects, unable to understand them or their ways. Or life.

One year, an earthquake suddenly destroyed the palace and many of the buildings in his kingdom. The king lost all the trappings of power, and his wife and children, within a few minutes. The royal city lay in ruins.

Then an old sage he had met earlier again appeared by his side.

"What are you going to do?" asked the sage.

The king, desperate and angry, shouted, "I've got nothing left! All my money is buried deep beneath the palace; I can't pay the soldiers, who are looting the city. I have no idea the state the rest of China is in. What can I do?"

The sage showed him how to build anew. He pointed to the fruit on the trees that would feed the emperor. He said, "Water to quench your thirst." And everywhere lay wood and stones in the rubble—to build with.

"Use what is there," the sage advised him. "Most people never see that. They go through life looking for something else, convinced that their objective is very distant when the things they need to achieve their aim are all around them."

And the emperor began to rearrange the rubble, stone by stone, with his own hands. Soon others pitched in. Before long, life had returned to the city, and everyone in it was making good use of every minute.

You also can enjoy a better life, in both a material and spiritual sense.

So what will you do with your hands?

Life here does have a purpose, for it gives each person a chance to learn the duties and joys of becoming a Co-worker with God.

17

Are Right and Wrong a Part of Spiritual Law?

E very religion has rules for living. They are the moral codes that keep order among the members of a society, rules for right and wrong behavior. In a Christian society, the basis for these rules is the Ten Commandments, a set of you shalls and you shall nots.

Moral codes provide a base for ethics, the discipline that deals with what is good or bad and what a person's duty is to others.

Society, over time, then develops a body of laws that try to enforce its moral codes and set of ethics, because good laws try to insure peace and stability within the social order. But people are people. During certain periods of history, the bulk of the laws are just. However, when a society drifts from an instinctive sense for the spiritual Law of Karma, which sets the highest standard for right and wrong, then the laws become unjust.

The laws are unjust because the people themselves are unsure about right and wrong. The leaders of such a society merely reflect the spiritual ignorance of the people. A society with poor leadership has only itself to blame.

What makes it so hard to determine right and wrong is that they are only an imperfect mirror image of the spiritual Law of Karma. True, the holy books may give the law in exact terms. Yet when the leaders in politics and religion don't know or understand the full impact of karma, they begin to cut corners, gnawing away at the laws that once insured a strong, peaceful, and fulfilling place for the people.

In times when people know and respect the spiritual law, their plan for getting goods or property is like this: "I want, therefore I work." After the majority of people forget the higher laws, they say instead: "I want, so I take." Human law is all too ready to support their greed, because its officers also have largely forgotten the once-honest nature of their duties.

A small book with a clear insight into how a society's laws develop in line with the laws of karma is *Whatever Happened to Justice?* by Richard Maybury (Bluestocking Press). Each society has its own history of how common law developed there. For example, the collapse of the Roman Empire led to the beginning of the Dark Ages around A.D. 500. Barbarians had the run of Europe. They set up feudal governments. These were small kingdoms under the rule of a king or lord who taxed his subjects at will. Luckily, the rulers were lazy. So they did not interfere in the lives of their subjects too much, as long as the latter paid their taxes, helped fight battles, and the like.

The lack of interference by the ruler was good, for the most part. Yet not if his subjects had a dispute. He usually did not provide for a court system to settle a dispute, where two parties could bring their grievances for a hearing and get justice.

But the Law of Karma is already in the hearts and minds of people. They need but listen for it.

The common people in the Dark Ages had that innate sense of right and wrong, so with their support a system of scientific law began. In his glossary, Maybury defines scientific law as the "verbal or mathematical expressions of Natural Law [divine law]." It is "learned through observation, study and experimentation." In the United States, for example, law today is merely political law, which he defines in the glossary as made-up law: "Same as legislation. Human law. Might makes right."

In the Dark Ages, a dispute between two people easily turned into a fight. After a bloody nose or two— or worse—the commoners began to look for a better way. Friends or relatives might advise them to find a neutral third party, often a clergyman. He would listen to both sides of their story, and after consulting some moral guideline, perhaps the Ten Commandments, he would issue a verdict.

The logic behind the decision was simple, says Maybury. But he added: "The fundamental nature of homo sapiens doesn't change much; what was right yesterday remains right today. Notice the emphasis on basics, on eternal truths."

There is much more to say about this subject, but Maybury found that common law, which common people developed from an attempt at justice during the Dark Ages, evolved from two basic laws.

The two laws are these: "(1) Do all you have agreed to do, and (2) Do not encroach on other persons or their property."

Maybury says that these two laws are the only ones that all religions agree upon, and thus are the basis for scientific law, which is a more accurate mirror of the Law of Karma than political law. The Higher Law is their basis. Beyond Higher Law, he recognizes

a Higher Authority, his name for the Divine Force—
God, the Holy Spirit, or some other deity, depending
upon the culture.

The spiritual value of *Whatever Happened to Justice?* is in the link it makes between the laws of earth
and heaven. For a member of ECK, it shows the
importance of life on earth. Life here does have purpose, for it gives each person a chance to learn the
duties and joys of becoming a Co-worker with God.

Obey the two laws above. They will guide you to
an upright life, opening doors to the spiritual knowledge beyond.

God, through Light and Sound, speaks to us in direct and indirect ways. The evidence is all around us, so much that we no longer notice.

18

What We So Far Know of God

Many speak of God like an old friend, but how many actually know God?

Most of us think we know our mate, whom we can see, touch, love, and perhaps argue with on occasion. But how often do we find just the right gift for our sweetheart — if, in fact, ever? Does that reveal how little we know about our loved one?

Despite any doubts we might have about pleasing someone we live with, talk to, cook for, or clean up after (or vice versa), we are usually proud of our knowledge of God. Yet how many of us have ever felt the full, raw brunt of God's love? And is this God Beyond All *(a)* a male, *(b)* a female, *(c)* a neutral force, or *(d)* all or none of the above? In some far corner of earth, at least one group of people is sure to endorse even choice *d*.

So what do we know of God?

God is not an old man or a giant in the clouds, whose passion is the vices of the human race. If God understood us as poorly as we do our own mates, the Last Judgment would have taken place centuries ago.

Is the God of All a He, a She, or an It? God is

beyond any such description of gender. God is not exactly an "It," but this tag works as well as any in our language to describe the Source of All. God made us, loves us, and preserves us. Many authorities in old church history have tried to paint this God like a folk hero: a being of the most noble virtues. But does a blend of traits whipped up by the limited perceptions of the human race actually show the real God of All?

There is no question of the existence of God. God is, and God is love. And that simple truth has more than taxed the limits of nations—at least if we study the texts of history.

Two ideas are key to why there is life and why it continues to exist. The first is that God exists. This Being, who is beyond human understanding, is the first cause of all creation: the universes and the beings in them. The second idea we must know to understand our world is that God speaks through the Word, which we call ECK.

What is the Word?

The five opening verses of John 1 in the New Testament give as clear a description of the Word, the Holy Spirit, as we are ever likely to find in world literature.

> In the beginning was the Word, and the Word was with God, and the Word was God. The same was in the beginning with God. All things were made by him; and without him was not any thing made that was made. In him was life; and the life was the light of man. And the light shineth in darkness; and the darkness comprehended it not.

The Bible does well in telling us about God and the Word, but it gives only half the picture of what divine nature is. An important point is certainly that it is *life* and that *"the life was the light of man."* However, there

106

is another side to the divine equation.

Besides the Light, there is the Sound.

The Sound. It is the missing half of what most people don't know about God and the Holy Spirit. God is what God is. However, we do know that God speaks to us through the Word—Logos, ECK, Holy Ghost, Comforter—and It communicates with the whole universe through the two aspects of Light and Sound. This is the secret of the ages. God, through Light and Sound, speaks to us in *direct* and *indirect* ways. The evidence is all around us, so much that we no longer notice.

Thus, the Voice of God is Light and Sound.

When It speaks through the Light, It uses any form or means that relies upon Light for existence. The artist, for example, may paint with a swirl of colors from a palette of mixed reds, yellows, greens, or blues. With these shades of light, he creates a picture for us to share a dream of inspiration. Such art lifts us spiritually.

An artist whose work has left many in a state of awe, love, or humility is Leonardo da Vinci, whose *Mona Lisa* gives a smile that hints at the mystery in divine love.

The mystic Blake, poet and artist, could also image the Timeless One. Blake's metal-relief etching *Europe, A Prophecy; the Ancient of Days* shows an old man, naked, with white hair and long beard blowing to the right, stooping in a circle of *light.* His vision of God is more narrow than da Vinci's. Blake, a recluse, felt that the power of reason was not the key to inspiration, but rather that the imagination and having access to the "inner eye" was the highest anyone could go in coming to an understanding of life. And so the old person in Blake's etching is reason, a mere shadow of God.

The ancient Greeks tried to show the whisper of God's Voice in their temples and statues. The Parthenon is a prime example of architecture that tries to express the divine qualities of light, beauty, and grace. Greek statues are also superb. The qualities that show up in the design of the temples also appear in the statues of Zeus, Apollo, Nike (goddess of victory), and Aphrodite (goddess of love).

So the Light of God plays upon our senses through any form that we can see.

The other way that the Word of God speaks to us is through Sound, or the vibration of moving atoms. It is God's unknown voice. This part strikes our hearing or sense of feeling, and the art form that reflects it most directly is music. The Psalms of David are songs of love for God. So, too, were the melodies sung in the early Catholic Church by a cappella voices, which in turn were incorporated into the Mass.

A certain group of people hear or sense the Voice of God mainly as Sound. These are often musicians. They feel a desire to reply to the Divine Sound inside them, which they know as actual sound or rhythm, by writing or playing music.

We all have our favorite music. It may range from a classical piece by Bach to "Amazing Grace," a tribute to God born of wonder, humility, and love by the onetime slave runner John Newton. Whatever our song, we are trying to say thanks for the love that God first gave to us. A mother's lullaby is a love song. The sweet talk of lovers is an offering on the altar of God's love, and so, too, the melody of a songbird.

God thus speaks through Light and Sound. People, in turn, reply to the Word through their art, sculpture, music, dance, crafts, writing, and all other forms of behavior. God acts, we react.

Why the Light and Sound of God? It is simply for this reason: The Light shows us the pitfalls on the road to God, while the Sound urges us on to our true spiritual home.

So what do we know so far of God? Enough. Enough to find our way home.

Life is about spiritual growth. We need to give our best in all departments of our life.

19

How God Speaks to Us, and How We Respond

Perhaps you've heard the story about a worker with years of seniority losing a promotion to a newer employee. In a rage, the older worker stormed into the manager's office to complain.

"Don't forget," he barked, "I have twenty-five years of experience under my belt."

The manager sat back in his chair. After a few moments of reflection, he leaned forward and said, "No, you have had one year of experience twenty-five times."

This is a story about a drop-off in spiritual growth. The main point is not about winning or losing a promotion, but about a person who kept missing chances to give to others at work. The missed promotion was Divine Spirit's way of reminding him of the Law of Cause and Effect. The man had lost his drive. It finally came down to his manager having to explain to him the reason a more qualified person got the promotion. Long ago, this worker had stopped giving his best. How many years had it been since he came to work with the thought of making a difference in the company that day?

Life is about spiritual growth. We either seize the

opportunities that life offers to become Co-workers with God—by learning to serve others—or we think mostly about getting our own satisfaction.

How does this story tie in with how God speaks to us?

God speaks through the voice of conscience, holy scriptures, feelings, and even the positive urgings of other people. Yet there are other ways. God's Voice also reaches us through human love, intuition, dreams, the Spiritual Exercises of ECK, or a direct experience with the Light and Sound of God.

The above story about the disgruntled worker is an example of the Divine Word speaking through the manager. A key purpose for life here is to have as many opportunities as possible to learn the give and take of divine love. What has that to do with the workplace? We must eventually learn to treat other people as lights of God too, giving love and respect to the spiritual side, a real chore when tempers clash. Even more, we need to give our best in all departments of our life. To avoid that responsibility is to drop back in spiritual unfoldment.

Our workplace, homelife, church attendance, school life, and many other interests can reveal valuable insights about our response to the Voice of God. Our goal in ECK is simply to become more aware and grow spiritually. A Co-worker with God does that.

God speaks, but do we listen? If so, how suitable is our response? The worker in the story above lashed out at others for his failure to grow spiritually, but isn't that usually so?

The Creator, the Highest Being, speaks to creation through the Holy Spirit, the ECK. This voice of divine love is very real. Those who enter the higher reaches of heaven here and now in their states of consciousness see the holy Light and hear the divine Sound of God clearly in everyday life. The Light and Sound are God's way to communicate directly with us. They help develop our creativity, which makes us godlike.

Showers of love rain down upon us simply because we are Soul, a divine spark of God. Its Voice, which showers the love, is the pure Light and Sound.

Most people are unaware of this spiritual gift. Indeed, they respond to the Light and Sound of God indirectly by listening to their intuition, trusting their feelings, or following their conscience. But others do see the Light directly; It often appears before the Sound. They are two parts of the Voice of God, the ECK, which speaks to all whose spiritual eyes can see the mysteries of divine love.

One day, a husband and wife were discussing a recent, unethical dealing he had had with a person outside the household. A true lover of God, he felt deep remorse for a thoughtless act committed in that dealing. Walking to the window while talking to his wife, he looked outside and saw the whole neighborhood bathed in a bright, shimmering pink light. The display lasted for some time. Finally, he called his wife to the window, for he wondered what could have caused this brilliant array of light. She saw nothing. As he continued to watch, a big ball of pinkish light shot upward and burst into small bits, like a spectacle of fireworks.

His unkind deed of the day had set off feelings of sorrow. He loved God, but his behavior didn't reflect that. He then realized that his past efforts to merit divine love were small and local in light of the monumental and universal love of God for him. That realization came on the heels of the supernatural pink light of God. The color pink is from the Astral Plane, the source of emotions and many problems.

The experience filled him with the humility and will to be a better person.

Very few people actually know how God speaks. Usually, even the most religious people can only "feel" the divine presence—at random times—yet they have very little understanding of how to listen to or see the Voice of God actively. So they often fail to respond to It.

A woman recently had a brush with death after she became ill with toxic shock syndrome. The disease began to get the better of her. At one point, her feet became numb, her blood pressure fell to a dangerous level, and the pain was nearly beyond endurance.

A team of young doctors set to work to save her life.

The night her illness reached a crisis, she felt very afraid of sleep. She thought it necessary to stay awake to survive, and that night proved to be the longest of her life. To make it till morning, she made up a Spiritual Exercise of ECK. She imagined herself in the company of the Mahanta (the Inner Master) and other ECK friends. She saw herself relaxing in their arms. The exercise was simplicity itself.

Later she made up other exercises that included the HU, an ancient name for God, which she sang repeatedly.

The night passed, and the illness with it. This crisis brought her a realization about the Spiritual Exercises of ECK: It took a real effort to create them during this emergency. She then realized the value of doing them daily—before the onset of trouble. Waiting until the hour of desperation could be too late. As it was, it still took her a lot of imagination and effort to create them during the pain of her illness. But her daily practice of the spiritual exercises had made it easier to reach for the love and support of the Mahanta and other ECK initiates.

The experience was a crossroads for her. In the future, she plans to give up several negative traits that have held her back spiritually and put more energy into higher ambitions. It's a far better response to the Voice of God.

God is always speaking to us and all life through the Holy Spirit. Like the worker mentioned at the beginning of this chapter, it is easy to forget Its guidance when we've strayed far off the path to becoming a Co-worker with God. A lost job, illness, and a hundred other problems are often a secret message from the ECK to turn us back to God.

Listen to God's Voice. Respond to It spiritually and know that despite every appearance to the contrary, all is well and in its rightful place.

Soul Travel has a lot to do with getting interested in things, starting with the physical world.

20

Small as a Thimble?

As an ECK initiate, who was gripped by fear, so aptly said, "If I'm so afraid of meeting the challenges of this world, how will I ever be brave enough to explore the God Worlds?"

Fear is a condenser; love, an expander. This means that fear can create a world as small as a thimble, while love is able to open us to the fullness of living. It is one thing to know this, but quite another to apply it to our life. The reason is, problems steal up on us. By instinct, we react with fear, hardly ever thinking to take charge through the spiritual aids available to us.

One resource we can use to expand our worlds is to call on the Mahanta, the Inner Master. As the Godman, he is always ready to help us win over trouble. But we must remember to ask for his assistance.

On occasion, adversity comes in the guise of interference from an inner source. Whatever we call this opposition, it cannot be dealt with by physical means. That leaves a person in a difficult position: either to accept the annoyance or to come up with an unusually creative way of solving it. The latter is the course chosen by the ECK initiate in the following story.

She was a homeowner who was moving into a new house purchased from an estate. The previous owner was a woman who had developed Alzheimer's disease, a degenerative disease of the brain cells that produces a general mental impairment. The victim was practically a vegetable and had been placed in a nursing home.

Late one night, the new homeowner was quite alone, sanding the floors and ripping up old vinyl in the house. Suddenly, as she was ready to head for the basement, she felt an aura of bitter hostility surround her. Immediately she thought of the Mahanta and the twelve ECK Masters who had been coming to her off and on for the last eighteen months. They appeared on the stairs and trooped down into the basement with her.

All evening long the waves of hostility swept at her. It occurred to her that the malice could be from the previous owner, who might have come in her Astral body to check on what she thought was still her own house. Naturally, it would make her angry to see a stranger tearing up the floors.

When the new owner returned to her old place to pick up more belongings, the Mahanta flashed a message through her mind. Speaking for himself and the other twelve ECK Masters, he said, "We'll stay up tonight and cleanse the place of negative influences."

The next day, the new owner found not a shred of anger or hostility anywhere in her new home, even though she worked alone until midnight.

In fact, she had an inner conversation with the former owner. Asking to be called Ruth, the woman said, "No one ever bothered to explain what's been happening to me. But now I understand. You're welcome to do anything you please with the house." No one had thought to explain to her the arrangements for the sale of her home, because she was a "vegetable" and would not have understood.

The ECKist overcame her problem by expanding her awareness to a higher level. The Mahanta was at hand, willing to stay the night and explain things to the victim of Alzheimer's disease. Once he had performed this simple courtesy, she had no further reason to obstruct the life of the ECKist by making unwelcome visits in her Astral body. The ECK student had been able to receive help because of her willingness to go beyond her thimble-sized resources to ask for help.

The Mahanta, the Living ECK Master may also use an everyday experience to give a person spiritual insight. This is called a waking dream.

A boss's son was getting married. The boss asked an employee, who was an ECKist, and another woman to decorate the reception room on the morning of the wedding. The room was on the fifth floor of a hotel, and the ECKist thought: *Just like the Soul Plane—on the fifth level.* She arrived at the hotel with a heavy box of ribbons, paper wedding bells, balloons, and table centerpieces.

She punched the "up" button on the elevator. When the door opened, she stepped in and hit the "five" button, smiling at the symbolism of riding to the Soul Plane in an elevator. It seemed a very quiet ride. Then she looked up at the lit floor number above the door and saw the elevator was still on the first floor. The elevator would not move.

She opened the doors and stepped off, thinking the elevator was broken. Next she climbed a staircase. It happened to be a false set of stairs, made only for a fashion show. At the top of the staircase was a platform that did not go anywhere. Again she was baffled as to how she would reach the fifth floor.

Following this, she went outside and climbed five flights of stairs. At the top, she found the door locked. At this point she started to sing HU, the love song to God, to calm herself. She then turned around and descended the stairs. At the bottom was a man wearing an all-blue uniform—a security officer. He unlocked the elevator for her so it would go to the fifth floor. "They lock it at night to stop vandalism on the other floors," he explained. She was now able to proceed to the room and begin decorating it for the wedding.

Suddenly she realized that neither her physical body nor Soul could get to the fifth level without the assistance of the right one to unlock the elevator door. The man in blue symbolized the Mahanta. The wedding on the fifth floor denoted Self-Realization. By means of a waking dream, the Mahanta had expanded her spiritual universe to something larger than a thimble.

He did the same for another individual, giving her a Soul Travel experience when she was afraid to have one.

In ECK one learns the principle that if he's not going forward, he's surely going backward. This chela was satisfied with her life. Her dream life was active, and she could recognize the Holy Spirit (ECK) at work in her daily life. And most of all, she was seeing the Light and hearing the Sound of God. Yet she recognized a complacency in herself; maybe she did need to learn Soul Travel.

She became like a fresh student, starting all over, working step-by-step with the spiritual exercises. She disciplined herself to wake up in the middle of the night to record any dream impressions. Like a child always keeping her parent in sight, she looked for Spirit in everything.

At this point, she realized she wanted God-Realization more than anything else in the world. Then came the Soul Travel experience. It was tailor-made exactly for her.

She awoke in bed, hearing her husband talking loudly in the hall and bumping the bathroom door with his foot. It annoyed her. Then with a start, she noticed he was also lying in bed beside her. Her first reaction was panic. All that moved were her eyes, gazing back and forth from the hall to the bed. Calming down, she thought: *After all, he's out of his body; not me out of mine.* But the Mahanta was gradually preparing her for what was really happening.

Next she felt herself floating upward into another dimension. It was like turning up a dimmer switch in a darkened room; it revealed the scene of an old general store. In her waking life, she had a weakness for exploring every old general store that came along.

This store was clean and bright. Her two young daughters, dressed in old-fashioned attire, were sitting on bar stools eating ice cream. The Mahanta spoke softly to her, "Look around." Still timid, she turned her head slowly. It was comforting to see the Master and her two daughters in the store, but she also needed the comfort of her physical body and the presence of her husband beside her in bed. So she was able to go back and forth between her bed and the Astral Plane, where this Soul Travel experience had taken her.

Again the Master said, "Look around." *Now this is real freedom,* she thought. Then, ever so gently, she floated back to her body, retaining the love and joy of the experience.

Whispering her thanks to the Mahanta, it occurred to her that he had been kind enough to start her with an old general store, which keenly interested her.

Then it struck her: Soul Travel has a lot to do with getting interested in things, starting with the physical world. This gives the ECK more to work with. And if one is truly interested in something, how can there be any room for fear?

Good-bye, thimble! Hello, worlds of God!

In the traditions of some Native Americans, the hawk is a messenger of God. Its appearance is a blessing, for it alerts an individual to go to the spiritual mountain and employ the gift of godlike vision.

21

Cry of the Hawk

In the seventeenth century, the philosopher Descartes said, "I think, therefore I am." That view is still appropriate for anyone who relies upon mental powers to approach life, but there is another, better way: the use of one's imagination.

I can imagine, therefore I can be more.

An imagination that develops along spiritual lines is by far of a higher, finer nature than anything the mind can produce. While the mind, at best, is like a surgical tool, the imagination is like the breath of God: able to touch the crown of heaven while in the most stricken of human conditions.

During one of my recent Soul journeys into the spiritual worlds, a dark speck appeared high in the heavens above me. It proved to be a small hawk in a steep dive. Coming straight toward me, it veered at the last possible instant, then flew in a circle around me. In the traditions of some Native Americans, the hawk is a messenger of God. Its appearance is a blessing, for it alerts an individual to go to the spiritual mountain and employ the gift of godlike vision.

A hawk is a good spiritual omen.

According to Native American legend, the hawk's cry—a shrill whistle—is to pierce the awareness and awaken people to a state of full awareness. The whistle of a hawk is like the cry of a prophet. In ECK terms, it is the voice of the Mahanta, the Living ECK Master, who comes to warn initiates about the hidden, unexpected traps of life. Even more, the Mahanta serves as a guide on the road home to God.

So the symbol of a hawk is about having a clear spiritual vision.

This image refers to an overview of life, which people can achieve when they learn to invite the Mahanta, the ECK, and Sugmad (God) into their state of awareness. It begins with imagination but ends in hard reality.

As a child, a certain ECK initiate we'll call Sally had problems with her right foot and leg that ranged from sprains to serious injuries. In some cases, she had even needed surgery. Today, married and working as a secretary, she finds her old nemesis of a weakened limb returning to make life as a wage earner more difficult. She recently sprained her right ankle again. To cheer her up, her husband brought home an orchid with nine flowers in full bloom.

An hour before dinner, Sally had finished her monthly initiate report to the Mahanta. The report allows the free use of imagination, to view life from every angle and then try to sort the problems into some order. Sally used her imagination to detail her frustration with work and the distress that her sprained ankle was causing.

After dinner that evening, she and her husband drew their chairs close to the orchid to do their daily ECK Spiritual Exercise. As they admired the plant, tears began to well up in Sally's eyes. The word *de-*

fective kept coming to mind. She felt defective in her own eyes and thought that the Mahanta and Sugmad saw her that way too. The couple began to sing HU, an ancient name for God, a simple yet beautiful song of prayer.

Her state of awareness began to open to a past life. Born somewhere in the Middle East, she was then a boy with a clubfoot and a deformed right leg—the same side as her pain in this lifetime. Her family in that life had left her in the desert to perish. However, a caravan came along to rescue her, only to enslave her in cruel surroundings. Sally recalled that past life as one of pain and severe hardship, for her rescuers treated her like a defective human being.

Those strong feelings of being defective carried over into the present life.

They also accounted for her feelings at work, where she thought of herself as only a secretary, doing menial work. It made her angry and impatient with her employer. The sense of being a slave nearly crushed her spirit at times.

Two days after she wrote her spiritual report to the Mahanta, in which she had asked to understand her feelings of inferiority, her ankle began to heal at last. Then also came a recognition of the spiritual value of her secretarial duties at work. They were giving her strength for the next portion of her journey home to God.

The Master's response to her letter, which she had written but not yet mailed, was like the cry of a hawk: a sharp whistle that cut through her self-pity by waking her to a higher state of awareness. He had let her see a past life. It gave meaning to what felt like undue pain and drudgery in the present.

Moreover, it was the gift of the orchid that had

opened her heart, for healings occur easiest in an atmosphere of love.

Use imagination in your initiate reports, dreams, and contemplations, for the Master's hawk appears to those who live by the precept: I can imagine, therefore I can be more. The sharp whistle of a hawk is one of the best images to appear in your spiritual life, for it holds out an offer of love, wisdom, and spiritual freedom.

Listen for its cry tonight.

When Divine Spirit sends a blessing of love to us, we must pass it on to someone else or suffer a reversal in spiritual growth.

22

Treasures Lost and Found

The gift of life is a treasure. What we do with our lives determines our spiritual state and our degree of contentment. While we in ECK can have and enjoy the material pleasures of life, we also know that all earthly goods carry a price and last but so long. And it is easy to lose them. On the other hand, real treasure often turns up in unexpected places.

In *Selected Fables,* the French writer Jean de La Fontaine tells of a man who put such a high value upon his material goods that in the end they owned him.

This miser had amassed a fortune in gold, which became his only source of pleasure. One day, fearing thieves, he carried this treasure to a distant place, digging a hole for it near a stone marker. He was always thinking about the gold. Whether waking or sleeping, eating or drinking, or going about his usual business, the cache was foremost in his mind. Often, in fact, he would visit that spot. He would circle the area by the stone, smiling, confident that the treasure was safe for him alone. But he had no plans to use it.

Eventually, a ditchdigger noticed the miser's

peculiar habit of circling the stone and shrewdly guessed that a treasure lay hidden there.

The gold disappeared, of course.

When the miser later returned, he found a mound of dirt and an empty hole where his gold once lay hidden. Crying, tearing at his hair, he mourned the loss of his treasure to a passerby.

"Somebody has taken my treasure," he wailed.

"Where was it, then?" asked the passerby.

"Right by that stone."

"Good Lord, are we at war that you should have had to carry it that far to conceal it?" asked the other. "Wouldn't you have been wiser to have kept it at home in your den ready to hand for the daily occasions when—"

But the miser interrupted the passerby. "Ready to hand? Heaven forbid! Do you suppose that money returns at the same rate as it goes? I never used to touch it."

"Pray, then, explain why, my dear sir," said the other, "you're in such evident pain over losing what you never used to touch. Bury a stone there—it's worth just as much!"

* * *

Life on earth is very exacting in the lessons it teaches about the Law of Cause and Effect. It's the old principle of an eye for an eye, and a tooth for a tooth.

Yet life has more to offer than the rigid Law of Karma, which by itself would make life here a miserable existence indeed. Karma is exacting to the letter. All who live under its law (which includes most of humanity) find that everything has a stiff price tag or some other penalty. Yet there is a balance even to the

132

Law of Karma—that of love. In essence, it means that when Divine Spirit sends a blessing of love to us, we must pass it on to someone else or suffer a reversal in spiritual growth.

We cannot bury the blessings of God in some dark hole simply for our own gratification. The Law of Love says to pass them on.

Where and how do the divine treasures come about?

* * *

La Fontaine tells another story that gives the source of most good fortune. A rich old farmer lay near death, so he called his sons to him to give them a final blessing. With his last breath, he gave them both a warning and a promise.

"Never sell the heritage that is yours by birth and was mine through my father and mother," he said. "Somewhere or other a treasure lies hidden in that earth."

Though he confessed ignorance about the location of the treasure, he urged them to finish the harvest, then dig up the land with plow and shovel in search of it. So when he died, his sons did that. They put their plows and shovels to the land, turning every inch. At harvest the following year, the land produced a bounty of crops and grains, though his sons never found a buried treasure trove.

Of course, the old man was wise. With his dying breath, he had taught his sons a golden rule: Work is the hidden reward.

* * *

A final story from La Fontaine is of a cobbler and a businessman. A poor cobbler sang all day while making and fixing shoes. Every morning, his happy songs disturbed a wealthy businessman nearby who was trying to catch up on sleep lost to worry over business matters.

One day, the businessman called the cobbler to his mansion. How much did the cobbler make each day? The cobbler scratched his head and said, "Sometimes more, sometimes less. So many holidays nowadays keep us from work. They ruin the trade."

The rich businessman thought it a quaint answer worthy of reward.

"Today," he said, "I plan to give you a throne." With that, he handed the cobbler a hundred crowns, a huge amount of money that represented a few centuries of labor for a poor cobbler. The cobbler's eyes lit like two lanterns.

Taking the fortune, he rushed home and buried it under the floor of his home—and with it also his peace of mind. No more did he sing his happy songs. Now his mind teemed with wild suspicions about neighbors and strangers who might that very moment be hatching some plot to rid him of his treasure. Every creak at night he imagined to be the stealthy footsteps of a thief. No longer did he sleep in peace.

In the end, the former cobbler ran to the mansion with what remained of the treasure and threw it at the businessman. "There, you keep your hundred crowns," he shouted. "And give me back my songs and my lost sleep!"

* * *

Make of these stories what you will. However, the real treasures of heaven are in your heart, not in your wallet. Seek and enjoy the gifts of life, but don't make the mistake of letting them own you and your peace of mind.

Dreams are a window to heaven. They link the two realities of heaven and earth — and allow you, as Soul, to move freely between them every single day when going to sleep.

23

Your Dreams—
A Window to Heaven

Dreams are a window to heaven. They link the two realities of heaven and earth—and allow you, as Soul, to move freely between them every single day when going to sleep. Unfortunately, most people care too little about their dreams, and as a result, their existence is both drab and spiritually poor.

For years, dreams have provided me with a wealth of insight. They have given clues about the motives of people around me, events in my life, and even about matters of health.

Of course, health is a very personal issue. We all have a different level of tolerance for various types of food based upon our age, the conditions under which the food grew, and the amount we eat. At times, in spite of our best efforts to take better care of our health, a physical ailment comes along that defies any attempt to correct it. Yet sometimes we can get an answer in a dream.

An example is the time I ate at a restaurant and became very ill from the meal. My wife and I had ordered the same lunch, but she had no reaction to it. As soon as we got home, I lay down for a nap. PeddarZaskq came on the inner planes to warn that my body could not now tolerate onions, though I had eaten them all my life. Since then, to test the dream information, I have cautiously placed an order for onions on several more occasions while out to a restaurant. Each time, onions have caused a quick, negative reaction.

Dreams have helped me understand other health problems as well. A few years ago I noticed that my handwriting was steadily growing worse, and eventually it became hard even to hold a pen. No amount of vitamins helped to ease the stiffness in my fingers.

During an inner experience one night, an ECK Master said, "You'll want to look at fruits. Those with a high acidic content may give some people the symptoms of arthritis."

Since then, I have cut back on some of my favorite fruits, like apples and oranges. Although I still eat them on occasion, I reduce the amount whenever there is less flexibility in my fingers, or when the joint of my big toe hurts. At other times, a sign of too much acidic fruit in my system is a pain or weakness in the knees. Whatever the pain, it always shows up in the joints. Immediately, I examine my diet for foods that are highly acidic and quickly change my foods until later when I can tolerate fruit again.

Adoni (ah-DON-ee) is a young ECK Master who serves among the nomadic tribes along the Indo-Asian divide. With dark and luminous eyes, he stands about five feet eight inches in height, is slender, and has quick and sure movements. His special interest is plants and herbs. In a dream, he once showed me certain plants in the wilderness that are nature's salt, pepper, and sugar. The nomads use these plants to flavor their meals. Adoni, though cheerful, is at once all business.

For other pains in the extremities, such as in the

feet or hands, another ECK Master once cautioned me about drinking too much gas-charged water.

ECK Masters like Adoni, Peddar Zaskq, and others are there to teach people in the dream state, ready to show them the way to wisdom, truth, light—and even to better health.

Do you want to know your place in life? Then study your dreams.

Much of the anger and hatred in society is due to a neglect of the inner life. Many people believe that a trip to church, a synagogue, or a temple once or twice a month is all that it takes for spiritual growth. How wrong they are. They need to grasp the spiritual nature of dreams, which can provide each with an open window to the causes in his or her life.

One has merely to watch the behavior of people to know that a strong reliance upon outer worship is seldom enough to cause a turnabout in consciousness. Church services alone do not improve the spirituality of anyone, for it also takes an equal amount of inner self-discipline, like contemplation, prayer, or a study of dreams.

The dream teachings of ECK can add a new dimension to your spiritual life. Here's how:

Whoever wants to unfold into a better spiritual person must always keep the name of God upon his lips and in his heart. The most ancient and holy name of all for God is HU. Sing this word often. Sung silently or aloud, it will stir the eternal force of divine love within your heart.

In time, your dreams will change. And if you love God above all else, you will develop spiritually in ways you could never imagine today. With a fresh spiritual outlook, your joys and expectations also will reach a new pinnacle.

The secret of happiness, as so many others have already found, starts by watching the parallels between your dreams and everyday life. That will be your proof that dreams are truly a window to heaven.

"Can one who loves life be ashamed of it?" Chuckling softly, he said, "Let me ask you again, but in another way. Do you love me?" The hobo was in fact the Mahanta, the Living ECK Master in disguise.

24

"Do You Love Me?"

Life is for living. Often, however, a block that we cannot dislodge by ourselves falls in our way. When the Mahanta, the Living ECK Master sees that we are powerless to deal with it alone, he may provide us with a new outlook. As a chela years ago, my short-sightedness revolved around a misunderstanding about the purpose of the ECK teachings. To me, they meant Soul Travel.

The fact of God's love never entered the picture, perhaps because I had so little love for myself.

When Jesus said, "Love thy neighbor as thyself," he meant that one must first learn to love himself. While a Christian, I had missed that distinction in his teachings. Later, as a member of Eckankar, I continued to overlook that finely shaded understanding. Accepting a new Master—the Mahanta, the Living ECK Master—had made only a slight change in my deep-rooted beliefs. The same need to live life with my heart instead of my head was still present. Of course, I did not know it then.

The Mahanta often comes to teach in a disguise. He, like truth, must slip up to the individual unrecognized.

If people see him coming, they put on their social masks, which prevent truth from entering into them.

One particular day in late summer of 1970 was like an oven. For months, I had lived and worked in and around a small Midwestern city. The face of Paul Twitchell, then the Living ECK Master, kept coming to mind. In early spring, he had been on hand for my meeting with the magnificence of God. For weeks following that experience, my life had been in upheaval, like a newly plowed field.

My destination was the bank, which anchored the main intersection downtown. It was payday, and I headed to the bank during lunch to deposit my check. Businessmen in light summer suits were hurrying to nearby restaurants in packs of twos and threes. Women moved smartly in high heels, doing errands and snacking on the run. By one o'clock, employers in shops and offices wanted to see them at work again. I watched the crowd flow like water on the street, people running in and out of buildings. The mobile crowd was like a living thing. Meanwhile, Paul's image remained strong. Why was he so on my mind?

My banking finished, I strolled to the pedestrian crossing to wait for the traffic light to change. People on the corner with me, on the way to important meetings, were like restless race horses at the starting gate.

Some time had passed since my experience of God on the bridge. That experience, arranged by Paul and the stranger, is told in *Child in the Wilderness*. It uprooted all that had ever meant anything to me and set it on end. Since that upheaval, however, I had retied most of the loose ends, settling into a new routine. But I was still struggling to find new values to replace many outgrown ones from my past.

Shame was a hurdle I had yet to leap. I knew the

ECK teachings about Soul were true because of my experiences in dreams, contemplation, and Soul Travel. Yet a dark side of the great leveler, the social consciousness, still festered in me like an angry boil. Unconsciously, I was ashamed of ECK. As an ECKist, I had learned many things about the spiritual worlds that had never entered my mind as a Christian. Despite that knowledge, I was ashamed of Eckankar, of its teachings, and even of the Mahanta, the Living ECK Master. But I didn't know that.

The traffic light turned green. The crowd lunged across the street. However, I chose to go at my own pace, steady and unhurried.

Without warning, a hand gripped my elbow. It was a hobo in baggy jeans and a faded blue cotton shirt, both items of dress years out of date. He had decided to accompany me across the street. Three days' growth of beard and a slouch hat set him apart from the citizenry, and his head just reached to my nose. There was something familiar about him, but I couldn't place it. I stepped up my turtle's pace.

"What's the hurry?" he complained.

The other pedestrians had already reached the other side of the street. The light was about to change again, but we had yet to reach the middle of the crossing. A motorist inched his car into the crosswalk, gunned his engine, and honked for us to hurry.

Danger from jittery motorists was but one concern. People knew me in this town. What would they think of my rubbing elbows with a hobo? When I tried to shake his hand from my sleeve, he simply gripped it tighter. His deliberate gait was more suitable for a walk in the garden than for Main Street at noon. My efforts to be free of his grasp seemed not to bother him at all.

I looked around nervously, but no one, except maybe the drivers, seemed to even notice us.

Then he asked, "Can one who loves life be ashamed of it?"

Life is a pretty broad subject to cover while crossing a street. So I cautiously replied, "Only if he lives a shameful life."

"Very good. Tell me, what is a shameful life?"

"Doing something you're not proud of."

"The question is not of *doing*," he said, wagging a finger under my nose. "It's a question of *being*."

"Being?"

A screech of brakes interrupted us. Cars from across the street had accelerated with the green light, but found us in the crosswalk. Drivers leaned on their horns.

The hobo, unmindful of the chaos, stroked his chin thoughtfully and asked, "What is life for, unless to make humanity more godlike?"

"Come on," I said, yanking his arm. "These guys'll run us down!" He set his feet, but I easily dragged him to the safety of the curb. Drivers shot us dark looks as they sped off. "You nearly got us killed!"

"What are you afraid of?" he asked.

Glancing at my watch, I saw lunch hour would be over in a few minutes. The proofroom supervisor expected me at my desk by one o'clock.

"Fear and shame are two sides of the same coin," said the hobo. "Either can shut out love. But you can be sure of one thing, even the lowest kind of love reaches for the heights of God. How can anyone live a complete life until he learns to love himself and his Creator? Tell me that!"

Anxious about the minutes slipping by, I was really more worried that an acquaintance might spot me with the hobo.

"Look, I've got to run."

"Remember what I said about love," he said. "Your life will never be right without it. If you say you love someone or something, show it. In giving love, you become it. That is how to become godlike."

He then gave me an odd, searching look that laid bare the deepest part of my heart. "Let me ask you a question," he said. "Are you ashamed of me?"

"Of course not!" I stammered.

"Then let me ask you something else," he continued. "Can a heart filled with love embrace fear or shame?"

Then he paused. His glance swept the street with its shade trees lining the sidewalks and its little patches of green lawn wedged in by concrete. Chuckling softly, he said, "Let me ask you again, but in another way. Do you love me?"

His question caught me off guard; it even made me a little angry. How could I love a stranger? From my view, he certainly was not a choice example of humanity. Love was for people you knew well, and even then, what could hurt more than a love betrayed?

"You're asking too much," I said.

"Love me and my words," he replied, "for I am always with you."

Quickly he turned and disappeared into a store. I stood fixed to the spot. Only then did it occur to me that the hobo was in fact the Mahanta, the Living ECK Master in disguise. Paul had come in his Soul body to speak to me of divine love. If I loved God, the ECK, and the Mahanta, then how could I be ashamed to walk beside a hobo? In what other ways had I hidden my feelings and beliefs, so others might not find the Light and Sound?

Through this experience with Paul, I learned that

147

love must first begin in our own hearts. If we can love ourselves, we can love the divinity of even a hobo. And only then can we rightly claim to love God.

In a bright ball of light, like a large sun, she saw the face of the Mahanta. "Don't be afraid," he said. "You will never be lonely again, for I am always with you."

25

The First ECK Initiations

The teachings of ECK offer a whole new world to the individual who wants to find God. And the ECK initiations are among your most valuable aids on this direct path to God.

What is an ECK initiation?

It is simply a spiritual rite that brings you closer to ECK, the Holy Spirit. There is no use of water, as in baptism. Nor a laying on of hands. Rather, the aspirant meets with an ECK Initiator, to whom the Mahanta gives the power to carry out this sacred trust.

Who, then, gives the real ECK initiation?

The Mahanta, not the Initiator, makes the actual linkup between Soul and ECK. In this regard, the Mahanta is the sole agent of God, for he is an Adept of the highest order—able to reach all levels of heaven. He is the Master of every universe. At home in the Far Country, he travels from the Physical Plane to the Ocean of Love and Mercy, and beyond. He has the wisdom and power to protect the neophyte in ECK, as well as any Higher Initiate.

The Mahanta, the Living ECK Master, holds the key to Sugmad.

What about the First Initiation? When can a new member of Eckankar expect to get it, and how does it come? The First Initiation takes place during a member's first year of study in the spiritual works of ECK, and the only witness is the Mahanta (the Inner Master), who performs it. It always occurs in the dream state. Bear in mind the purpose of the ECK initiation: to give you a closer bond with Divine Spirit.

So open your heart to love.

For an idea of what to expect in the First Initiation, let's glance at the dream journal of Gene (name changed for privacy), whose heart was open to divine love.

Gene sat in a comfortable chair at home, did a Spiritual Exercise of ECK, and fell into a light sleep. In a dream, he met the Mahanta, the Living ECK Master. Gene had asked to sign up for a discourse, so the Mahanta was taking him to an ECK center on the inner planes. The center was in a large building.

Inside, behind a desk, sat a woman who helped Gene register for an ECK Satsang class, a system much like the one used to sign up for a course in college. The Master then signed the papers to authorize Gene as a bona fide student. Next, Gene received a symbol. It was a key of sorts, in the shape of a pair of pliers, which could help him identify the correct scrolls of truth, the real from any imitation ones. The key would also let him gain access to secret materials of ECK.

Gene awoke from contemplation. He knew that his dream had been the First Initiation in ECK. Any fear he might once have felt about this holy ceremony had left, replaced by the warm and gentle love of the Mahanta.

What about the Second Initiation?

Many High Initiates still recall the Second Initiation as if it were yesterday. The Second, unlike the First, is a dual initiation in that it occurs on both the inner and outer planes. Sometime go to the indexes of *The Shariyat-Ki-Sugmad*. Turn to the sections in the two volumes that relate to initiation, for the subject is well worth your time.

It takes most people two years of ECK study to qualify for the Second Initiation. The ECK Spiritual Center then sends a notice of invitation, which the individual is free to accept.

What can you expect at the Second Initiation?

In the outer rite, an Initiator gives the person a secret word to sing during a spiritual exercise. The word is also for protection. The inner half of the Second Initiation may occur before, during, or after the outer event, but it is the latter that counts as a valid initiation here. And each initiation is unique, though there is a similarity among those of the same circle.

This story is of Lynne. Again, it is not her real name. She told of this experience in relation to the inner part of her Second Initiation.

Lynne had been eager to receive the initiation for some weeks, but she had a few worries about whether she would recall it later. Not everyone does. Sitting in silence, she began to chant her word softly for a few minutes, when suddenly a stream of bright light flooded her Spiritual Eye: the Light of God. With It were three ECK Masters. First came the ECK Masters Peddar Zaskq (the spiritual name of Paul Twitchell) and Fubbi Quantz, abbot of the Katsupari Monastery in northern Tibet. The third figure was a monk in a brown robe.

Then came a scene from the past. A small child in a green dress was playing in a cornfield with the three ECK Masters. Lynne had a recollection of herself as a child wearing that dress. A summer storm rumbled on the horizon, but since the storm was still at a distance, the child kept playing in the sun.

A voice said to her, "You will always live in the sunshine."

The scene shifted to the initiation again, and now a bright ball of light, like a large sun, appeared. Then she saw the face of the Mahanta. "Don't be afraid," he said. "You will never be lonely again, for I am always with you."

In the final scene of her Second Initiation, Lynne saw a monastery high on a cliff in the far distance. It was the Katsupari Monastery. "If you ever have any problems, go there," the Mahanta said. "Go there; the answers will come." And her initiation was over.

Who can fathom the power and love of God?

The ECK Temple at Chanhassen, Minnesota, is the fifth major Temple of Golden Wisdom on the physical plane. The other four exist on a supraphysical level, meaning they are only visible through the Spiritual Eye.

26

The Temple of ECK

An important date in the history of Eckankar is May 22, 1989. On that day, the city council of Chanhassen, Minnesota, approved Eckankar's request to build a spiritual edifice. This edifice is the Temple of ECK.

The ECK Temple at Chanhassen is the fifth major Temple of Golden Wisdom on the physical plane. The other four exist on a supraphysical level, meaning they are only visible through the Spiritual Eye.

The first temple, in the Gobi Desert, is called the Faqiti Monastery. The grey temple is rectangular, topped with a broad dome. Wide steps lead to the main portal, which is flanked by high, square columns. Banjani, the ECK Master in charge, teaches the introduction to the Shariyat-Ki-Sugmad. Students come here in the dream state to learn their spiritual destiny.

A second Temple of Golden Wisdom is hidden in the remote Buika Magna mountain range of northern Tibet. This is the Katsupari Monastery, founded by Rama. It is near the Valley of Shangta, gathering place for the ECK Masters at the passing of the Rod of ECK Power. Legend says that Jesus once came to the monastery during his "silent years" and met the ECK Abbot Fubbi Quantz.

Chief among the writings in the Katsupari Monastery is the first section of the Shariyat, "The Chronicles of ECK." The Kadath Inscriptions, also found there, provide a historical record of the Living ECK Masters throughout the ages. The Records of the Kros, another set of old documents, relate the history of earth and prophesy its future. Years before the Chinese invasion of Tibet, intrepid travelers sometimes came to Katsupari for the Kaya Kalp treatments of physical rejuvenation.

Gare-Hira is the third major Temple of Golden Wisdom on the physical plane. It lies concealed in the remote Hindu Kush, in the spiritual city of Agam Des. Agam Des means "inaccessible world." This city is the home of the Eshwar-Khanewale. Called God-eaters, they consume cosmic energy much as we eat food.

The Temple of Gare-Hira is a white structure that looks somewhat like an Islamic mosque. It is a sturdy building with a white dome topped by a cupola. Classrooms ring the main sanctuary, and the second section of the Shariyat-Ki-Sugmad is displayed on the altar of the inner sanctum. This section is called "The Records of the Kros." The ECK Master Yaubl Sacabi is the guardian here, and students come nightly in their Soul forms to study the wisdom of God.

The fourth Temple of Golden Wisdom on the physical plane that interests us is the House of Moksha, in the city of Retz on Venus. *Moksha* means spiritual release from our lower bodies. This temple is a dome-shaped structure of a translucent material that echoes of the Sound Current. Rami Nuri, the ECK guardian here, teaches the third section of the Shariyat to all who come in their dreams or by Soul Travel.

158

Chanhassen is the site of the fifth main Temple of Golden Wisdom on the physical plane. It sits on a large tract of land in Chanhassen, Minnesota—a suburb ten miles west-southwest of the twin cities of Minneapolis–St. Paul.

The Temple consists of three linked areas: the Temple, an administration office, and a spacious vestibule. All three are modified octagons. The Temple itself is a two-storied building roughly twice the size of the administration office and seats eight hundred in the second-floor sanctuary. For special events, temporary seating on the first floor has room for several hundred more people.

A pale golden ziggurat crowns the Temple. The stepped, pyramidal roof is reminiscent of architecture common to ancient Sumer, Babylonia, and Assyria. The design symbolizes mankind's spiritual journey up the plateaus of life. Humanity starts at the level of human consciousness and makes its deliberate way to the top of the summit and God Consciousness.

Square pillars adorn the outside of the Temple complex, which is set among rolling hills. A public lake touches Temple property on the west.

A search for the ECK Seat of Power had been under way since at least 1980. On January 27, 1980, I saw the future site of the Temple in Minnesota. The Vairagi Order felt an urgent need to find a permanent location for the Temple of ECK and the Seat of Power. It is the central vortex from which the Mahanta, the Living ECK Master gives the ECK message to the world.

The guardian of the Temple of ECK in Chanhassen is, of course, the Living ECK Master. The Temple is a gathering place for inner and outer study. Acolytes and initiates come here physically, in the dream state, in contemplation, and via Soul Travel to study the holy works of ECK. ECK worship is provided for the public and ECKists who choose to expand their states of consciousness. HU Chants for initiates are also conducted here, as well as ECK Satsang classes.

Paul Twitchell foresaw a Seat of Power years ago. He said it was to be like the Vatican in Rome or the headquarters of the Mormons in Salt Lake City, Utah.

In *Letters to a Chela,* he said: "It is a law of these worlds that for a teaching to survive, the movement to be preserved, there must be an established seat of power from which the thought forms, energies, and power flow. When Eckankar was small, the seat of power existed wherever the Master resided. This has to be changed due to the scope of the activity and the exposure of the teachings."

It was a rugged assignment to accomplish the initial planning and land approvals for the Temple of ECK. A small, dedicated team of ECKists and non-ECKists helped to realize the goal. The first part of the task was thus achieved, but then came the larger, more difficult assignment of actually building the ECK Temple.

Paul not only spoke of a Seat of Power, which combines the ECK Temple with an administration office, but he also foresaw a place to put all the official buildings, the archives, and a spiritual city. That larger vision belongs to the distant future. For now, we have simply built the Temple of ECK. The rest can be done in its rightful time.

"Those who cannot work on the active outer works for the sacred spiritual city," he continued, "will be doing just as much in laying the cornerstone for this phase of the works by giving small or large donations. Each stone and nail and square inch in this complex is spiritual history, is blessed, and so will be those who brought it about for the generations of spiritual pilgrims to come.

"The child who saves ten pennies for such a labor of spiritual love has done as much as the adult who gives his month's salary."

The ECK Temple is the spiritual center for Eckankar missions. The temple focuses our efforts as never before. If you have helped in this project, you receive the blessings of ECK in ways beyond imagination.

By helping to raise the Temple of ECK, you have helped shape the destiny of Eckankar.

In the act of giving you will find a sense of spiritual unity with others. Get into the habit of giving. It will bring you more spiritual fulfillment and a greater state of consciousness.

27

The ECK Temple:
A Gift to the World

The dedication of the Temple of ECK on October 22, 1990, opened a new page in spiritual history. The Temple is a gift for all whose search for God has met failure in the past. However, the Temple of ECK is also to renew the spiritual life of one who is already in Eckankar.

So the ECK Temple is God's gift to the world. To understand what this means, let's consider a few points about it. What, for example, is a seat of power? What role does the Temple play in the spiritual quest of people? And to whom is it dedicated?

What is a seat of power? Does it take the place of the Rod of ECK Power? Does it add to or subtract from the duties of the Mahanta, the Living ECK Master?

A seat of power is an organization's connection with the world. An actual place, it links a group with everyone outside itself and comes in many shapes and sizes.

A place where many people live is a city, with a group of leaders in charge of its government. The building that houses its leaders is city hall: a seat of power. In baseball, a team like the Minnesota Twins connects with its fans in the Hubert H. Humphrey Metrodome in Minneapolis. That stadium is a seat of power.

Likewise, people who worship God meet at a church, synagogue, or temple. Catholics and Protestants in a community gather at their respective church on Sunday. Jews come together in their synagogue on the Sabbath. ECKists will also meet at the ECK Temple for their own special times of worship and fellowship.

Each church, synagogue, or temple is thus a seat of power. Each is a center for its members to make a link with the outside world—from which to teach, to serve, and to love others.

So, too, the Temple of ECK is a spiritual center from which to tell others about the Light and Sound of God.

Yet, it does not replace the Rod of ECK Power, the spiritual authority which the Sugmad has given to the Mahanta, the Living ECK Master. Think of the Rod of ECK Power as a column of Sound and Light that gives him direct access to the Sugmad. This line of communication with God goes everywhere he does. The Temple of ECK, however, is but one instrument which the Master uses to bring the message of Light and Sound into the world. It, of course, stays in one place.

In 1972, Dorothy found her way to Eckankar. It was a year after the translation (death) of Paul Twitchell. The ECK books, discourses, and other teachings inspired her, but something bothered her about the ECKists. Why was the ingredient of love so often missing among them? She saw divisions, deep conflicts—and ECKists showed disdain for each other. She found their behavior quite out of keeping with the teachings of Eckankar: a path of pure, divine love.

Yet, through the years, the ECK has carried her through many problems and sorrows. She is happy to see this new cycle of growth in Eckankar, which includes the building of the ECK Temple. This new cycle welcomes all.

The Temple of ECK is a gift to the world in that it will bring a spiritual healing to many. Already, the world has seen sweeping political changes, a sign of inner changes that have preceded the outer. The human race is not yet ready to give up hate, but many survivors of its barbaric acts are now ready for the ECK teachings. There is a growing interest in Eckankar by people who used to live behind the Iron Curtain and the Berlin Wall.

However, the Temple of ECK is also a gift of healing for ECKists. Dorothy had also noticed a sense of isolation among a number of ECKists. They had misread the scriptures of ECK and so cut themselves off from the rest of the world. They selected those parts of *The Shariyat-Ki-Sugmad* that spoke of the individual, the Chosen People, and our last lifetime on earth. In their lopsided selections, they separated themselves from God's other creations. And so they were often lonely, filled with disdain, and critical of one another.

This pall of isolation stopped the rise of spiritual fellowship among ECKists. Too many were looking for an angle where ECK would serve them: not how they could serve ECK. Their strong drive to be individuals actually made them withdraw from others. They called it detachment. That led to a spiritual drop-off: to unhappiness and failure. In their one-sided selections from *The Shariyat,* they had completely overlooked the balance of becoming a Co-worker with the Mahanta and Sugmad.

165

Far too few in Eckankar knew how to accept gifts from the Holy Spirit and return them to others.

The Temple of ECK can bring a healing in Eckankar such as never seen before. Because of it, many will learn how to pass along the gifts of ECK to others. The Temple will help develop a stronger spiritual bond among the members of Eckankar. It will be a center from which the message of Light and Sound will reach many seekers in the world.

Behind the stone, mortar, wood, and glass of the ECK Temple is one purpose: to give the ECK teachings to all who want them. Helping with this mission can be your gift to ECK.

I dedicated the Temple of ECK to the Sugmad, the ECK, and the primordial Mahanta. So also will all true initiates of Eckankar dedicate themselves to the service of God. They can make this spiritual commitment during their first visit to the ECK Temple, and also during each later visit.

The ECK Temple is a gift to the world. However, it will take your many gifts of love, service, and donations to keep it here. It is also in the act of giving that you will find a sense of spiritual unity with others in ECK. Get into the habit of giving. It will bring you more spiritual fulfillment and a greater state of consciousness. Yet, let your gifts be pure, and always from your heart.

The Temple of ECK is thus in the service of God. It stands as a beacon of divine Light and love, for both you and the world—a gift to all.

Personal experience with the Light and Sound is leading many to the certainty of truth and the shortest route to heaven.

28

The Seat of Power

Building the Temple of ECK is an important milestone in the history of Eckankar. At its dedication, the ECK Temple became the Seat of Power, our spiritual center on earth.

Why a seat of power?

It is a law of the physical world that for a group to survive as long as possible, it must set up a seat of central government. For religions, this center is the hub for its spiritual activities, administration, and culture. Rightly or wrongly, people consider their seat of power the most important place on earth.

History gives many examples of seats of power.

Five to six thousand years ago, the ancient Sumerians built temples for their gods and goddesses in every village. Sumer was where Iraq is today. Villagers believed that the deities who lived in these temples protected them. By 2000 B.C., the capital city of Ur had constructed a temple called a ziggurat. It was a tower made of mud bricks, which narrowed at the top like a pyramid. The roof of the ECK Temple is reminiscent of this ancient design.

Babylon was another seat of power in Mesopotamia.

About 600 B.C., King Nebuchadnezzar II built an ornate temple there, also a ziggurat. He dedicated it to Marduk, chief god of the Babylonians. Babylon remained a center of politics, religion, and culture until 539 B.C., when the Persians captured it.

There is a reason for this short review of past seats of power. Many ECK chelas of today lived in those ancient times. They farmed the rich soil in the valley between the Tigris and Euphrates Rivers. As the population grew, they built towns and cities, and temples within them. Soldiers, traders, merchants, housewives, and children—their seat of power gave them all a sense of purpose and well-being.

A seat of power is often at a crossroads. The ancient Peruvians had such a place in the Andes from about 800 to 200 B.C. At 10,000 feet, they built Chavín de Huantar, a holy city and ceremonial center.

Pilgrims came for miles to give offerings of llamas, food, and ornate pottery to their gods. Set in a mountain valley, Chavín de Huantar was at the confluence of two rivers, tributaries of the Amazon. The city linked the trade routes of mountain villages and coastal settlements. People came there to worship, but also to trade goods and handicrafts. Some of today's ECKists who lived then got their fill of nature spirits.

However, after six hundred years, the spirit of its religion waned. Chavín de Huantar then disappeared as a force in history.

An example of political seats of power is the garrison towns of the Romans. The Romans expanded their empire across Europe during the first two centuries A.D.

Other seats of power common today are city halls and county seats, and the capitals of states, provinces, and nations. Nearly everyone knows national capitals such as Beijing, Bonn, Canberra, London, Moscow, Ottawa, Paris, Rome, and Washington, D.C. All are political centers. Each serves as a place of pilgrimage, a meeting place where its citizens can exchange ideas and goods, enjoy culture, renew friendships, and develop connections in business.

A seat of power is any place from which a group's energies and ideas may flow into the world. No seat of power is permanent. Sometimes a location may be a seat of power for centuries, but eventually a new force—perhaps climate or politics—causes people to settle elsewhere.

The nomadic tribes of Israel had no seat of power. In 1000 B.C., King David captured Jerusalem from the Jebusites (Canaanites). His son Solomon then built his renowned temple in Jerusalem, which became their seat of power.

However, Nebuchadnezzar II's army burned the temple in 586 B.C. Upon the Jews' return from Babylonian captivity, they began to worship in synagogues. Zerubbabel soon rebuilt the temple, but the synagogue had emerged as a center for Jewish religious, intellectual, and community life. It was a school, meeting place, and judgment hall.

Herod's temple replaced Zerubbabel's in about A.D. 64. A short six years later, the Romans burned it to the ground while suppressing a Jewish revolt. By now, however, the local synagogue had become the seat of power. Political upheaval was responsible for transferring the seat of power from a central temple to community synagogues. The synagogue is why the Jewish faith has lasted so long despite much oppression. Still, the synagogue did not replace the functions of the temple.

Many ECK chelas helped to write Jewish history

171

in past lives. Thus they understand that ECK centers and Satsang classes focus our spiritual activity as the synagogue does for the Jews. Despite these similarities, Eckankar is a spiritual hierarchy. The Mahanta, the Living ECK Master is the final authority for all matters of ritual, doctrine, or leadership.

A seat of power less well known to Westerners is the Muslims' seat of power, Mecca. It is the birthplace of Muhammad, whom they believe to be the last of God's prophets. Mecca is in western Saudi Arabia, fifty miles east of the Red Sea. Inside the city is the Haram (the Great Mosque). It, in turn, encloses the Kaaba, the holiest sanctuary of Islam. The sanctuary houses the Black Stone, the most revered artifact of Islam. Five times daily, Muslims must face toward it while praying.

Mecca is a forbidden city to non-Muslims. However, it is the chief destination for all Islamic pilgrims, for their religion expects all who can to make a pilgrimage there at least once in their lifetime.

Christianity, well known to us in the West, springs from the teachings of Christ. Yet it was Saint Paul's missionary work among the Gentiles that sparked its wide popularity today. Originally, the seat of power for Christianity was Jerusalem, because the first Christians were Jews. Over the centuries, Christianity split into three main churches: Roman Catholic, Eastern Orthodox, and the many branches of the Protestants.

Roman Catholics look to Vatican City as their seat of power. It is the seat of the church's central government, and the pope is the absolute ruler.

The Eastern Orthodox Church accepts many doctrines of the Roman Catholics. However, since their split in A.D. 1054, it has become the more mystical of the two bodies. It treats priests and laity as equals.

Even its titular head, the Patriarch of Constantinople, is simply the "first among equals." The seat of power for the Eastern Church is Istanbul (Constantinople), a city of more than six million inhabitants in northwestern Turkey.

The Protestants who broke from the Roman Catholic Church did so over the issue of good works. Martin Luther felt that good works alone were not enough to assure one of salvation. Like Saint Paul, he looked to faith as the key to heaven.

In ECK, we find that only the Light and Sound of God can raise us spiritually. An ECK initiate will certainly do good works, because the cleansing power of the Holy Spirit brings him compassion. Faith, however, is only the starting point in ECK. Personal experience with the Light and Sound is leading many to the certainty of truth and the shortest route to heaven.

Protestant denominations number in the hundreds. Each has its own seat of power, which communicates the unique beliefs and practices of its members to the world.

Why build a Seat of Power for Eckankar?

Like other religions or spiritual groups, we must have a home from which to reach out to the world. We need a place from which the Mahanta, the Living ECK Master can speak to the world about the Light and Sound of God. The Temple of ECK will become the chief destination of spiritual pilgrims the world over.

For now, the Seat of Power for Eckankar is in Minnesota. At the crossroads of humanity's quest for spiritual freedom, it is the spiritual center of the world.

Mainly, it is the starting place for Soul's dream of reaching God.

We do what we can to explain Divine Spirit's ways to each other through stories about ourselves and others. Thus, stories play a key part in kitchen-table conversations.

29

Kitchen-Table Conversations

The teachings of ECK will soon reach more people than ever. For this to happen, we must find a common language to speak with those who want to learn about ECK.

Think of having a kitchen-table conversation with a friend. How could you explain ECK simply over tea and doughnuts?

Many ECK initiates of tomorrow are still members of an orthodox religion today. They are your friends and neighbors. You've known some of them a long time, since before you came to ECK. Others you met later—at school, at work, or maybe in your community. Sooner or later, they will ask what you believe. How you tell them can influence their feelings about ECK.

An ECKist of ten years has grown close to several people through business and other activities. Most are devout Christians. It took awhile for each friendship to form, because they knew he was a member of Eckankar.

At first, there was mutual suspicion. They were wary of each other's beliefs, and whenever someone tried to bring up religion, it made everyone else squirm.

Slowly, they found a common language. Then respect began to replace fear, and tolerance overcame distrust. The common ground for their conversations now is dreams, spiritual attacks (instead of psychic attacks), having a spiritual guide, and the Light and Sound. The ECKist may also pass along a technique for spiritual protection, such as the "Mountain of Light." He shows friends how to find an answer to a problem by shining a light on it in contemplation or even by having them visualize Jesus.

An impasse is the word *prayer*. This ECKist wonders about the reluctance of ECK chelas to use it as part of a common language. Is prayer always an invasion? Many of his Christian friends use prayer to aid their own spiritual unfoldment: a proper use that creates no karma. While prayer is not the ECK chela's way of talking with God, one can pray rightly with an open and loving heart.

People have asked him, "Do ECKists believe in God?"

They had noticed a lack of spiritual terms in his speech when he purposely avoided ECK words, because they didn't know them. So he is right in suggesting that *prayer* can be a common-language word for "contemplation."

Through a friendship, the Mahanta showed him why prayer may be a better word to use than contemplation. A Buddhist friend does a chant as her prayer. It works for her, but it sounds odd when she says, "I chanted for such and such." He doesn't want to sound like that when talking to others about ECK.

So, in talking with those in orthodox religions about the spiritual exercises, you may sometimes want to use the word *prayer*. At least they'll understand you.

Later, you can tell them our name for it: the Spiritual Exercises of ECK, or contemplation. We need to change the way we talk if we are to bring the message of ECK to others. We want to build bridges, not walls.

This same initiate and another ECKist are business partners. One day, they had a meeting with their new marketing director and her graphic artist, both Christians. The four of them were designing a new brochure for the company. As the ECK business partners reviewed the first draft, they spoke of a lightness they always tried to have in their company's sales material.

One explained, "What we look for in the artwork and writing is Sound and Light." They meant the two ways that God makes Itself known to people.

Their guests took the statement in stride, so the speaker continued. He said they look for the Light in art as a lightness and openness. And they look for the Sound through the vibration, the quality, and the life of a piece. The marketing director and the graphic artist understood immediately. They did that in their professions, too, but had never thought of it in those terms.

Then the graphic artist asked, "Do you use this Sound and Light with other things, like food preparation?"

One of the ECKists said, "We use it for everything. We use it for business decisions, for keeping the energy in the shop clean and fresh, as well as for food preparation." The common language of Sound and Light made it easier for them to explain how much they depend upon ECK, or Divine Spirit.

Later in the meeting, the marketing director asked how the ECK partners had managed to get seven articles about their business into major newspapers

177

and magazines in the last few years.

"People pay us to get such connections," she said. "How did you get yours?"

"We have no connections with any of the newspapers," the ECKists replied. The marketing team was dumbfounded. Only half joking, the graphic artist quipped, "It's the Sound and Light. That's how they did it!"

Yet all four knew that was exactly how the ECK initiates had managed to get so much coverage in the press. For Its own reasons, the ECK had provided the ECK partners with free publicity. The marketing people could see that the ECKists had a special connection to this principle of Sound and Light.

These two ECK chelas like to see Eckankar taking its rightful place among the religions of the world. One said, "I've been an ECKist since 1980, and now the outer works are really starting to make sense and be real." They understand that Eckankar is a path for all and that some precepts of ECK are in all religious teachings. Why, they wonder, do ECKists sometimes feel the need to separate from life to live life?

What do they notice most about today's Eckankar? Simply this: "With the outer teachings blending more and more into kitchen-table conversations, life is getting richer every moment."

What is a kitchen-table conversation? It is a heart-to-heart talk with a friend about something that means a lot to us.

In ECK, we often try to understand why certain events occur. Why did the ECK let us have this or that experience? We do what we can to explain Its ways to each other through stories about ourselves and others. Thus, stories play a key part in kitchen-table conversations.

This article is a kitchen-table conversation between you and me about spiritual matters.

The goal of Eckankar is to bring word of the Sound and Light of God to all who are ready to receive it. Among other considerations, it means a change in approach. Yet some will hold on to old ways, even to the point of using ECK terms with people who know little or nothing about ECK.

For *Sugmad* say "God." Use everyday words in place of ECK terms when speaking to the public about ECK. It builds a common language. Without a common ground, we defeat our missionary efforts in ECK.

When telling someone about ECK, imagine yourself in your kitchen. How would you talk to a friend over tea and doughnuts?

You will find a kitchen-table conversation a good way to talk with others about the Sound and Light.

The great Tibetan ECK Master Rebazar Tarzs said to Paul Twitchell, modern-day founder of Eckankar, "We are not unfolding for the purpose of having our senses acted upon. We are unfolding to give all that we and our senses are capable of giving. Then shall our lives be transformed."

30

The Secret Side of ECK

A correspondent recently told of her concern about the direction of Eckankar: the ECK Worship Service and the missionary program. In her heart she couldn't support them.

Why, she wondered, couldn't she just go to the HU Chant and Satsang as before? Was it so important to do all this outer work? What was the reason for changing the way things had always been done in the past?

First, nothing is ever the same as before. Everything changes all the time. Second, many members of ECK have had problems because they provided no outlet for the gifts of the Holy Spirit. Third, ECK initiates can continue to go to HU Chants and Satsang classes as before, or study in private if they choose. The path of ECK is so broad that people can live the spiritual life of their choice. The Mahanta, the Living ECK Master has the duty to see that the teachings of ECK are available to all.

In time, an ECKist learns of the secret side of ECK. The Holy Spirit touches every living creature, all the time. Few people ever know that, but this knowledge is common to those advanced in the spiritual works.

Rebazar Tarzs, the Tibetan ECK Master, tells Paul Twitchell about the secret side of ECK in *The Key to ECKANKAR*. He explains how to become a Master. What is the purpose of spiritual unfoldment? How does the ECK transform a person who wants the qualities of Mastership?

Rebazar says to Paul, "We are not unfolding for the purpose of having our senses acted upon. We are unfolding to give all that we and our senses are capable of giving. Then shall our lives be transformed."

What will this changeover do for us?

The ECK Master explains further: "We shall realize all of the capabilities, all of the gifts, and all of the demonstrations of love which are radiated by those in the spiritual worlds. Then too will we be the master of our destiny, the master of our fate."

Rebazar Tarzs refers here to two kinds of people. One is happy with a solitary existence; the other wants to be a Co-worker with God. Some in ECK are unconsciously striving for the first choice: They want their senses acted upon. Others, who know the secret side of ECK, want to give all that they and their senses can give. The first group focuses on the individual in the ECK teachings. It accepts but holds to itself the gifts of Spirit. Those in the second act as Co-workers with God, passing along divine gifts to others.

Recently, a man gave me a precious gift: a small, well-shaped golden seashell that someone had given to him. He put it into my hands with care. As with all the many gifts from ECK, I tried to think of who would appreciate the full value of this gift. It will go to a woman who has treasured the beauty of seashells since her childhood.

Why pass to others the gifts of Spirit? A gift from

the heart creates a love bond between people.

Now, anyone who loves God is a channel for God. Most people who love God, however, are unaware of being channels. An ECKist, on the other hand, wants to be more and more conscious of how the Holy Spirit acts through him to touch life.

And yet, in the dialogue mentioned above, Rebazar gives Paul a word of advice: "One thinks that to be a saint or master, spirituality is the first and primary qualification. It is, but spirituality must not be regarded by the mind in such a way that we separate our ways or ourselves from those who do not know."

So how does this work out in everyday life? A Higher Initiate met a man successful in business who has little acquaintance with Eckankar. She told him about singing HU, the spiritual exercise that centers upon one of God's holy names. She told him how to do a contemplation.

"And look for a white or blue light," she added.

Some months later he called to tell her he would soon be in town on business. He also said the HU exercise wasn't working: no white or blue light.

Rather than take his statement at face value, something (the ECK) prompted her to ask him a question.

"So, what *do* you see?"

"Nothing but this small Chinese guy with a long white beard!"

She knew it was the ECK Master Lai Tsi. "I'll bring a picture of him when we meet for dinner," she promised.

"No, don't bring a picture," he said. "What if it's him?"

She brought it anyway, and he recognized Lai Tsi immediately. The Higher Initiate had mixed feelings about the connection between this man and the ECK hierarchy, because she knew what lay ahead for him. Humorously, she referred to the release of karma to come into his life as "the scrubbing and all."

Yet, she had done her part. She had acted as a missionary for ECK when the occasion let her tell this man about HU. The main difference between her and a lot of people, including some ECKists, is that she pursued his conclusion of apparent failure with HU. While he didn't see a blue or white light inwardly, the Holy Spirit did reveal Itself through an ECK Master. This Higher Initiate is a channel for God, but more aware than usual of the secret side of ECK.

The Holy Spirit is always working through us to uplift others. More often, It has people act on Its behalf though they may only have a faint notion about what is taking place.

An ECK couple in Canada recently took a trip through the major Indian reservations in the Canadian provinces. A hot issue just then was the political rights of Indians. Without knowing it, this couple stayed at the very lodge where Indian chiefs from all over North America were to meet a few days later. Following their vacation, the ECKists heard about the meeting and knew that the Holy Spirit had guided them to that location to prepare the ground. The Mohawk Indians soon after laid down their arms and gave up their barricades in all provinces.

One night after visiting the Indian lodge, the husband asked his wife why ECKists are often unconscious of activity in their inner world. How does the ECK actually use them as channels? Why are even ECKists so unconscious sometimes of what's happening in their own lives?

She happened to have with her one of the ECK

books by Paul Twitchell. In one place, Rebazar Tarzs tells Paul that often a chela is unaware of the implications in the world around him. He will not know outwardly why he meets a certain person or goes to a certain place instead of another. Yet, if one is open, the ECK will use him as a clear channel for Its purposes.

How can you begin to see the secret side of ECK?

First, know that ECK is behind everything. Second, learn to do one small deed for someone else each day, without any expectation of reward. Third, love God with all your heart.

Do this, and the ECK will show you Its secrets. You will then find love and become the master of your fate.

The ECK-Vidya is the ancient science of prophecy. It teaches you about yourself. What forces act upon you during this stage of your life, and what developments can you expect in the next one?

31

The 12-Year Cycle

One of the most interesting studies a student of spiritual matters can take on is a study of the ECK-Vidya and its 12-year cycle. The ECK-Vidya, of course, is the Ancient Science of Prophecy.

The principle behind the ECK-Vidya is simple. "Whosoever and whatsoever is born or done at a given moment of time has the qualities of that moment of time," said Paul Twitchell. This principle exists because of the system of order that exists in all universes, from the highest to the lowest.

The ECK-Vidya, Ancient Science of Prophecy by Paul Twitchell sheds a new light upon the reason for human existence. It teaches you about yourself. What forces act upon you during this stage of your life, and what developments can you expect in the next one? The ECK-Vidya can provide a lifelong guide to spiritual unfoldment. It works in unison with the Spiritual Exercises of ECK to reduce the effects of karma that cause the uninitiated person so much blind grief in everyday life.

First, what part does a 12-year cycle play in the affairs of an individual?

The 12-year cycle is a great cycle of the ECK-Vidya. Greater cycles include a factor multiplied by it, such as the 60-year cycle. On the other side of the equation, lesser cycles include the three- and four-year cycles. But the 12-year cycle provides a key turning point in the life of a person.

Second, where is the starting point of a 12-year cycle?

Start with a key experience in your life: birth, an illness, an occasion of good fortune, a change of occupation, a marriage. Begin with any life-changing event. That becomes the pivotal point from which to add or subtract the number twelve to tag a peak of experience, a twelve-year cycle. *The ECK-Vidya, Ancient Science of Prophecy* gives a chart of the ECK-Vidya Wheel for further study.

If you've chosen a true highlight from your past as a starting point, a similar pattern of intense experiences should become apparent after a study of the 12-year cycles in your life. For some, these cycles are easy to see. Others, who live less dramatic lives, may have difficulty in telling one 12-year cycle from the next. However, it is possible.

Finding the origin of a 12-year cycle is a valuable spiritual aid especially when one finds himself on the threshold of a new cycle. To illustrate, I will give an example from my own life.

A key 12-year cycle began for me in 1969, the year I took the Second Initiation. This was a very important event, for it meant the complete surrender of my inner life to the ECK, Divine Spirit. I decided to place my spiritual affairs entirely in Its hands. It was a moment to remember. However, I was very uncertain about taking such a step at the time, because the ECK teachings were still new to me. Was it the right step?

The Second Initiation means that a Soul makes a total commitment to follow the ways of Divine Spirit. Never make this decision lightly. In fact, coming from a strong Christian background, I shivered at the apparently reckless way I had put my well-being in the afterlife at risk. But the desire for God must be strong. If truth were so easy to get, then wouldn't everyone have it? Were that so, then all the great religions would have made earth a paradise many centuries ago.

But despite the best effort of these religions, earth often resembles the shades of hell.

Truth brings divine love. The reason for such human failings as war, theft, lies, and other natural traits of humans is that no religion can drive love into anyone's heart. When God's love enters the heart, only then can a change for the better occur.

The 12-year cycle is only a part of the ECK teachings. When people understand it, the Mahanta, the Living ECK Master can more easily help them open their hearts to the pure Light and Sound of God.

This Light and Sound equals divine love.

Briefly, here is a summary of one aspect of 12-year cycles in my life. It goes all the way back to when I was three—about the time a Soul makes the transition from the inner planes to life here in this world. Every twelve years since then has brought monumental changes in my life, as I go into a new and greater area of spiritual growth. At about the age of three I had rickets and whooping cough. In my midteen years I had lead poisoning that caused severe migraines. In the mid- to late twenties there was the upheaval in health that followed my Second Initiation. At the end of my thirties came the health crisis that preceded my accepting the Rod of ECK Power and the spiritual leadership of Eckankar.

In 1981, a 12-year cycle began with my appointment as the spiritual leader of Eckankar. Those twelve years brought great spiritual changes in every spectrum of life here on earth, in every area of human endeavor, including religion, politics, and economics. There were upheavals everywhere. Those twelve years showed that life is indeed a sea of endless change.

On October 22, 1993, another 12-year cycle began. Each time a new cycle occurs, Divine Spirit causes an entire revamping in my life, ranging from changes in outer conditions, health, and other aspects of the spiritual life. Each time a new cycle comes, I need to set aside time to adapt to the changes.

Now I need to prepare for the next 12-year cycle of service in ECK. It means taking care of my health, which I often neglected during the last cycle. This is necessary in order to set the pace for the next round of spiritual unfoldment both in the ECK circles and in the world at large.

Each 12-year cycle can mark a time of spiritual upliftment, if a person keeps his face toward God. It's a time to balance the rate of vibrations.

This short article is not a complete study of the causes and effects of a 12-year cycle, because the details vary with each person. The Mahanta can give knowledge. But knowledge is no guarantee that the individual who hears it will have the discipline to turn it into spiritual gold—the wisdom of God.

You will notice that the years I've given above sometimes occur before or shortly after the calendar date of a 12-year cycle. These great cycles blend into each other. Seldom is there a sharp break between one cycle and the following one. The changes bring a re-ordering of sorts, and the process usually lasts a year or two. Further, a reading of the ECK-Vidya is not absolute in its message about the future, because it lies within each of us to create a better future for ourselves through right spiritual action. Actions, after all, follow the prompting of the heart. If the heart is pure, so are the deeds that follow.

It is very helpful to study the ECK-Vidya. You will gain a better insight into the spiritual laws that underlie the movements of governments, people, and individuals. And you will benefit the most spiritually from such a study.

The Master endures suffering because of his love for Soul. All this is necessary for a transformation to lift the consciousness of people around the world (and everywhere else) to a new level.

32

Notes on Health and Healing

First of all, my sincere thanks to the many of you who sent love, tips, and information during my recent bout with illness. It shows that ECKists are up to date on the latest findings in science, medicine, and alternative healing. Mostly, though, thank you for your love and concern.

A chela asked a very good question.

She wanted to know: An ECKist with a certain problem, like a health concern, can go to the inner planes and ask the Mahanta for guidance to restore health. Why can't the Mahanta, the Living ECK Master do the same?

The answer: He can—if he puts his attention on it.

Paul Twitchell once mentioned some holy men who ended this life through disease, accident, or mischief on the part of enemies. Didn't these holy men know what the future held in store for them? Paul explained that a person who has his attention upon God and others most of the time, due to his personal mission, often neglects his own well-being. That is all too true.

For my part, I simply live in the arms of ECK, doing

Its will to the best of my ability. There is so much joy in giving service to Divine Spirit in dozens of ways that sometimes I neglect the obvious: to look out for myself.

Whatever the outcome of anything, my creed is this: Not my will, but Thine be done.

Once alerted to a problem, however, I can—and do—turn to all the available resources on both the material and spiritual planes. Of course, the further along a condition has gone, like poor health, the longer it takes to restore it.

It looks as though my recovery will take some time. This can affect my travel plans for another year or two, but I will do what is possible. Please bear with me.

This condition began to turn more serious in late autumn of 1993, even though traces of it had bothered me as far back as 1984. In my years of service in this position since taking the Rod of ECK Power in 1981, I have traveled to many places around the world to meet with as many of you as possible. The travel, food, and other stresses have taken their toll on my health over the years.

Fortunately, the basis and strength of the ECK teachings is the doctrine of the Inner and Outer Master, which means that I am always with you. When conditions keep the Outer Master from traveling, the Inner Master is always there.

I have met many fine healers during these long months of recovery. One of them is a Chinese acupuncturist. He trained in China as a medical doctor many years ago, but for his own health reasons, he became a practitioner of acupuncture. A holistic healer, he sees a unity between health, profession, and happiness. They must all work or there is an imbalance, he rightly feels.

A very practical man, he said, "Bad for health; bad for business."

He told of a Chinese man who got several million dollars in backing to build a Chinese grocery store that would specialize in preparing foods on the premises. They'd produce tofu and flour, for example.

After opening, however, the store got a bad reputation because its food spoiled uncommonly fast. Soon people stopped coming.

So the manager called in a monk who knew about good and bad energies and how they affect the environment. The manager wanted to know the reason his business was failing.

The monk went all through the store, looking at how the place was set up. Then he went outside. Pointing to some high-tension wires on tall towers over the store, he said, "That energy is bad!" Instinctively, or by training, he knew the dangers of electromagnetic radiation (EMR).

"Bad for health," he concluded, "bad for business."

Nonetheless, the Chinese manager had invested so much money in the store that he tried to stick it out. But somehow, the EMR from the high-tension wires overhead sped up the spoilage of his prepared foods, like tofu and flour. The losses mounted. One day, the manager simply disappeared, and the business failed.

Electromagnetic radiation, it appears, finally tipped the balances against me too. It causes a host of other problems: a poor assimilation of foods, weakness, and other more serious concerns. But I'm working on my health now. No computers, no TV, no microwave oven; limited exposure to fluorescent lights, telephones, airplanes, etc. It's a different world, a different life.

All this is necessary for a transformation to lift the consciousness of people around the world (and everywhere else) to a new level.

The Master endures suffering because of his love for Soul.

When Sugmad (God) created Soul, It put in each of us an unconscious desire for survival. In some, this instinct for survival is stronger than in others. The more spiritually advanced a person is, the more likely he is to do everything in his power to survive whatever outer conditions attack him.

Of course, the human body is mortal.

Each of us comes to earth with either a mission or a duty. Those who have advanced spiritually in past lives and wish now only to serve God, and other living creatures, come with that mission.

Most people, however, still have much to learn about the Law of Cause and Effect, and responsibility. They are very much under the Law of Karma. Their reincarnation is the result of having to fulfill a duty—in other words, bathe in the waters of unknowing and get a lot of experience. Much of it is lost on them. But in the next world after this life, the Lords of Karma review their past life with them and point out what the day-to-day lessons meant to them spiritually.

Yet that's how divine love grows.

If your troubles seem too much to bear sometimes, please remember that they are also giving you a greater capacity for love and compassion.

The lights on the map were Souls that the Mahanta had already made first contact with. "Reach the 33% who've already had an experience with the Light and Sound of God," Fubbi Quantz said.

33

The ECK Researchers

There is a saying in business that a company must reinvent itself every ten years or so to remain competitive. That's a good idea for a spiritual path, too, especially in today's climate of fast change in people's needs and tastes.

The truth about ECK initiates is that some are good Vahanas, or missionaries, and some are not. What makes the difference?

Take two ECKists who love to help with the ECK missionary effort. Both teach Satsang, both give ECK introductory talks; and both do radio, TV, and newspaper interviews. Yet one reaches the willing Souls while the other does not. What gives?

Both go through all the right motions. The first ECKist, the unsuccessful one, uses old techniques from ten and twenty years ago. He or she frightens people. There is too much emphasis on death and the journey into the other worlds, for example. Too much talk about the consequences of karma. Such topics put new people off today. It's OK to mention them—they are, after all, a part of the ECK teachings—but why dwell on them?

That approach is a *feature*-driven one. It pats *us* on the back about the comprehensiveness of our teaching. But it comes at the expense of the spiritual needs of the seeker.

A look at the second Vahana, the successful one, shows a very different pattern. He or she is willing to try new ways of reaching the millions of willing Souls, and works closely with the ECK initiates at the Eckankar Spiritual Center. This approach works. Its success lies in having the focus on the spiritual needs of the seeker instead of what a great teaching *we* represent.

So we call the second approach a *service*-driven one. It puts the seeker's spiritual needs first. We find here none of the vanity or self-service of Vahana number one.

Now a quick story to illustrate the scope of the ECK missionary effort.

A High Initiate who works closely with the ECK Vahana project from the ECK Spiritual Center had a vivid experience during contemplation. Wah Z took her to the Katsupari Monastery where Fubbi Quantz greeted her warmly. He took her into an enormous room full of spiritual beings from the inner worlds and other planets. Each worked diligently. They pored over volumes of books. Some of the pages were holograms, giving a three-dimensional view of the spiritual demographics of places by layers of feelings, memories, and thoughts.

And the holograms had maps. Some maps had a few sparkling lights on them; other maps had large clusters of them.

Fubbi explained, "The beings studying the holograms are researchers. They are pinpointing the best places to contact people who are ready for ECK."

The researchers did a thorough study of their areas. They looked at all the media. How would radio, TV, and newspapers respond to ECK in a certain area? By the way, the lights on the map were Souls that the Mahanta had already made first contact with.

Researchers also analyzed which areas had ECKists who would welcome and love the newcomers.

Fubbi added, "This is a worldwide, planetwide, innerworld-wide project. The researchers write down which media ECK Vahanas should try first and which areas would open up." A massive project.

"Reach the 33% who've already had an experience with the Light and Sound of God," he said.

Before leaving, Fubbi winked at her.

"In case you ever think you're doing this by yourself, remember that this is what's working behind the scenes. You're a physical vehicle, much appreciated, but it's definitely a team effort."

That was her experience during contemplation.

The entire ECK spiritual hierarchy is working on the ECK missions project. Your link with them is through the ECK Spiritual Center.

Work in harmony with the ECK and you'll find your efforts as an ECK Vahana to be surprisingly successful.

Should the ECK, or Holy Spirit, ever touch your heart, you realize there is never any turning back on the path to God.

34

Can You Ever Go Back?

The teachings of ECK help people deal better with the problems of life.

A woman from Nigeria often gets her guidance from the Mahanta, the Living ECK Master in dreams. Before a dangerous trip, she asked for his protection. In a dream, he gave his blessings: "Daughter, go in peace."

It was a safe and uneventful journey.

Once, tense from problems, she told them to the Mahanta before sleep and awoke with this song in her heart, "Let go and let God." Another time, he said, "Keep an ECK dream book, study your discourses, and always do the Spiritual Exercises of ECK." She heeds this advice. Her problems—both the material and spiritual—always find a solution one by one, for he's always near to give her strength and joy.

Can you ever go back?

Should the ECK, or Holy Spirit, ever touch your heart, you realize there is never any turning back on the path to God. Ever.

In a beautiful passage on love from *Stranger by the River,* the Tibetan ECK Master says to the seeker:

"Therefore, if you desire love, try to realize that the only way to get love is by giving love. That the more you give, the more you get; and the only way in which you can give is to fill yourself with it, until you become a magnet of love."

Love is the key to heaven.

As a member of ECK in Germany says: "What was once of utmost importance, interest, and necessity is fading away. What was in the beginning difficult with no entrance is now open and more easy." His new approach to living is due to the power of love he found in Eckankar.

The Mahanta, the spiritual leader of Eckankar, is the Dream Master. His sole purpose is to help people find spiritual freedom, and he often comes to a person in the dream state to give love, wisdom, and advice as needed. He and other ECK Masters often appear to Mary R. of New York.

They have shown her what love is and what love is not. At work, Mary used to care too much about social acceptance, even if it meant staying at lunch far beyond the usual lunch hour. She often ate with the office gossip circle. This "in" crowd fed upon the latest happenings at work, but Mary grew more and more uneasy in that group, so she finally quit going to lunch with them. But to reach that decision, she first had to deal with her fear of being an outsider. Now she feels more in balance and at peace.

Then she had a dream about fear.

Lai Tsi, one of Mary's favorite ECK Masters, often appears in her dreams to teach about things like love and fear. She loves him for his strength and gentleness.

One night Mary had asked for his guidance and ended up with a potent yet frightening dream. She dreamed she had brought home an inmate. She never thought of him as a prison inmate, but simply as a human being in need of food, shelter, love, and care. Later, her suspicions about him began to mount. Why had he been in prison? As her curiosity grew, so did his anger and ill-treatment of her. Then he had his friends over, and they disrupted what little peace remained in her home.

She awoke in a panic. Angrily, she asked Lai Tsi how he could have allowed her to have such a frightening dream.

Then she understood its meaning.

Lai Tsi had indeed been loving to her. He stood by, giving her protection, though he let her have a traumatic look at how fear was destroying her life.

Who was the inmate? He was a symbol for the energy current of fear she had been carrying with her for a long time. Mary had housed it, nurtured it, and slept with it, not fully aware of its basic negativity. Once she took note of its sinister force, it gained momentum and began to avenge itself upon her. Fear had always been a threat to her very existence and inner security.

All the attention she had showered upon fear had come back to her like a boomerang. It had been destroying her life. From that dream, she realized the need to get a grip on her fears if she ever wanted to find peace.

In the end, she was grateful to Lai Tsi for this dream.

From my window, I see a neighbor with rake in hand, cleaning up his yard. On weekends, he takes care of his lawn; during the week, he is at work.

Like most people, he thinks of himself as the caretaker of his home, his family, his lawn, and perhaps even a garden. But he is actually caring for himself. Each stroke of the rake and each turn of the shovel teaches him some vital spiritual lesson. When this stay on earth is over, his shovels and rakes will stay behind.

Only his spiritual toning goes with him.

Seize the moment, seize the day—and embrace life with joy and wonder. The ECK teachings offer you a simple way to enjoy life to the fullest measure: the Spiritual Exercises of ECK. Do them daily, do them well. For they bring love.

Once you taste the sweet nectar of divine love, you will move steadily ahead toward God—never happy with the old ways again.

You would never go back.

In the seeker Peddar Zaskq and the ECK Master
Rebazar Tarzs we find a classic example of the student and his mentor, a role model with great wisdom
and understanding.

35

Superman or Mickey Mouse?

The real topic is role models, not cartoon characters. But Superman stands for the ideal, the person who stands at the top of the pyramid in his field. And Mickey? Well, lovable as he is as a cartoon character, here he represents the bottom of the pyramid, and all those people who count themselves as failures.

The ECK Master Rebazar Tarzs and the seeker discuss this very subject in "The Law of the Self" *(Stranger by the River)*.

Peddar Zaskq, the seeker, says, "I have seen the struggle of mankind and the very control of their earth world destiny by individuals [the Supermen] who have control of their lives and the power currents."

But Rebazar corrects him.

"Thy vision has overlooked the fact that Soul is mightier than space, stronger than time, deeper than the sea, and higher than the stars."

Rebazar put the seeker's attention upon an overview of existence. While there are a few Supermen of some sort or another scattered about among humanity (the Mickey Mouses) in roles such as politics, religion, or even literature, that is only a human standard of high achievement.

There is a higher standard.

That standard is to become godlike.

Like the ECK Masters.

This earth has a very definite place in the spiritual education of people. It is somewhere between heaven and hell. Some of the experiences it has to offer can be joyful, heavenly: learning to give and receive love. Yet those experiences can also be hellish at first as an individual goes about it all wrong.

Heaven and hell here on earth.

Still, it is the many experiences of both kinds that finally convince a person that there must be more to life.

The seeker in *Stranger by the River* has done the right thing. In pursuit of truth, he has sought out the very best role model that Soul could hope to find: in this case, the ECK Master Rebazar Tarzs. The seeker actually has a strong desire for God. Who better, as a role model, than an ECK Master, who once also made his first halting steps to God Consciousness— but who finally reached it?

So in the seeker and the ECK Master we find a classic example of the student and his mentor, a role model with wisdom and understanding greater than, well, Superman.

And what does Rebazar tell the seeker?

"You, yourself, are your own problem," he says. "You must understand and act to solve the mystery of thy little self before you can solve the mystery of God."

What is this law? I have written and spoken about it many times in the past, but it is important for a very good reason. It marks the place where Soul begins Its journey home to God. Note that.

So Rebazar says, "This is the law of the Self—the law of God. Therefore, I tell you not to take up the seeking of God until the little self within thee is conquered and solved."

Some signs that the little self is a stumbling stone to one's spiritual desire for God include, as Rebazar points out, a greater sense of outrage over the faults of others than at our own. Excusing our own weakness and shifting our blame to others. Liking gossip.

You may ask, "Well, what am I doing here on earth?"

That's like a child in school saying, "What am I doing here?"

Earth is a classroom. Its purpose is to help people develop (usually after many lifetimes) a godlike character.

So earth is a classroom, a place of repetition. Way back in my first year of school, I distinctly remember how hard it was to remember all the pencil lines, intersecting at random, that spelled my name. How would I ever learn those curious, meandering lines? A mainstay of teaching—and learning—is repetition. So my teacher had me write my name ten or twenty times every day until the lines crossed and flowed in the right places.

Our spiritual lessons on earth come the same way. At first, our attempts at writing are without any direction, like a mouse fleeing in an oats field. But soon, after many failures, there is a slow improvement. It's not long before we can write our name, and a lot of other words, without so much as a thought.

So it is with karma. For example, we make a thoughtless comment about our dislike for someone, just as that person happens to come into the room and overhears our remark. That moment of embarrassment lives on. Imagine that your critical remark was about your employer. How will that weigh on the scales for your next salary review?

Earth is the place to air our mistakes.

The mind is a powerful tool or weapon, depending upon its use. People choose mentors, or role models, from infancy on to learn how to become more self-sufficient. A child looks to its parents. Students look to their teachers.

A woman who is an excellent cook and seamstress says she learned those skills from her grandmother. In basic military training, some recruits have never fired a weapon before. Yet a few of these earn a ribbon for expert marksmanship. They were people who usually excelled in other skills, too, because of having developed the habit of listening carefully to the advice of their instructors.

Earth is a place to develop our constructive skills, those which do good in the world instead of harm. The good skills develop one's godlike qualities, because to succeed with them, the individual must consciously or unconsciously come to respect the skill.

To obey a teacher exactly requires a lot of patience and self-discipline.

How do you know you are ready for ECK, the straight path to God? When you look at yourself and ask, like the seeker, "Can life be no more than this?" And if something inside you answers with a resounding yes, you are seeking the higher self, through ECK. It means you're ready to be something greater than Mickey Mouse or even Superman.

From that moment on, your search for spiritual truth has begun.

212

Then came a second dream. The Mahanta took him
on the Time Track and showed him a past life in which
he had been a woman.

36

Getting Answers from God through Past Lives, Dreams, and Soul Travel

Most all his life, a certain man harbored a stubborn fear of life. This fear robbed him of happiness and vitality, often leaving him angry and full of self-pity. He couldn't understand it or break its hold.

Years later, he became a member of Eckankar. His outlook on living improved in many ways after that time, but this fear of life remained at the borders of his consciousness, always ready to pour water upon the fires of his hopes and dreams. Then one day, he finally learned the reason for that haunting fear.

An Eckankar seminar near his home featured a HU Chant on Sunday morning before the regular program.

A HU Chant is a spiritual exercise. For a half hour or so, a group of people sing HU, an ancient name for God. It is a strikingly beautiful song, much like a Gregorian chant sung by a large group of singers.

Early that Sunday morning, about three or four o'clock, he had a dim memory of a dream about the ancient Mayans and a past life he had spent as one. But he fell asleep again and forgot the details.

At seven-thirty he arose, dressed, and traveled about forty minutes to the seminar. He put his attention upon "the Mayan thing" during the HU Chant.

His Spiritual Eye opened.

A past-life recall told him of another lifetime when he was a young woman among the Mayans. In that life, she was very beautiful. The beauty came of her intense love for life, which brought happiness and joy to everyone who knew her. Her very atoms breathed this exultation.

Unfortunately, her beauty also caught the attention of the temple priest, who always kept an eye out for human sacrifice worthy of the Mayan god whose stone image sat with cupped hands before the temple. The priest cut out her heart while it was still beating.

This man, looking back on that lifetime as a beautiful woman, now knew the reason for his fear of life.

Never since had he been able to recapture such a love of life. But he also realized the reason he had come to Eckankar—a chance to restore that love to his life. Yet the old fear always lurked in the shadows. All his life, he had the instinctive feeling a fatal blow would strike him if he ever again loved too much.

Singing HU had opened his heart to God.

In some way, God's love will open our hearts so that we have the courage to face the darkest secrets from our past.

God speaks to us through past lives, dreams, and Soul Travel. The above example illustrates how Divine Spirit, the Voice of God, told him the reason for his longstanding fear of life.

The play of karma underlies all human relationships.

In this next story, a young man gets to balance the

scales of justice from the past. He needed to repay a victim from a previous life, but the Mahanta, the Living ECK Master (the spiritual leader of Eckankar today) sent a dream to prepare him for the necessary, though painful experience.

Nick, a name we'll use to insure his privacy, had a dream in which a beautiful young woman came to the office. She was trying to use the phone on his manager's desk. Nick and the girl felt an immediate attraction for each other in the dream, and soon they began a passionate romance. But, to his frustration, it led nowhere.

Then he awoke.

Some weeks later, a young student came to the office to get work experience. Nick loved her from the start. He did everything in his power to win her heart, but she coyly brushed aside his passion with promises. Later, always later. Soon everyone in the office was talking about their relationship.

Then the sky fell in.

Through the office grapevine, Nick learned that this young woman had been having a secret love affair with his best friend at work. It had begun nearly the first week that she had arrived there. Worse, Nick had set the stage. One night that first week he had to work late, so he asked his good friend to take her home. That was the beginning of the end.

Only the ECK, Divine Spirit, kept Nick from losing his mind when he learned of the secret love affair. But he turned sour on life. Why had this beautiful young woman come—to purposely bring him grief?

In his anxiety and anger, he even forgot about the spiritual love of the Mahanta, the Living ECK Master.

Then came a second dream. The Mahanta took him on the Time Track and showed him a past life in which he had been a woman. Married to a wealthy man, this individual had two house servants, both of whom suffered due to Nick's misuse of position and authority. One was this student.

"You made that karma," the Mahanta explained. "That debt stands between you and God's love. Pay now and be done with it."

In the end, Nick recognized the hand of karma and the long, outstanding debt that he needed to settle. It took awhile for the crushing pain to subside, of course, but now he's happy he settled the debt. After the pain had finally gone, Nick felt a new sense of freedom and lightness. God's love could now shine more directly into his heart. That obstructing block of karmic debt was gone.

Dreams are thus a second way that we get answers from God.

What is Soul Travel?

Soul Travel is a more direct, conscious way to transcend the human consciousness in order to hear God speak through Its voice, the Holy Spirit. Most saints in history knew this ancient science of Soul Travel. They used it often during their prayers or meditations.

A very new member of ECK, Melissa (a pseudonym), did the Spiritual Exercises of ECK every day during her first two months of studying the ECK discourses. These are monthly lessons in the spiritual works that the Mahanta, the Living ECK Master usually sends to ECKists for the expansion of consciousness. Most discourses have a special exercise each month.

Melissa went into contemplation before going to bed. The Light of God filled her Spiritual Eye, and a few notes of music (the Sound of God) followed.

Then came the sound of rushing air or wind. She was moving in her true spiritual form, the Soul body. But suddenly doubt and fear filled her heart. A former Pentecostal, she immediately called out the name of Jesus. Things started to go in reverse. Where once she had moved forward, she was now traveling backward in the spiritual worlds.

Quickly, she caught herself.

Melissa told herself that she would put her complete faith and trust in the Mahanta. Again she moved forward. The lesson gained from this Soul Travel experience was that if she placed her trust in anyone other than the Mahanta, she would indeed regress instead of moving forward spiritually.

That is an example of Soul Travel. It was God's way of telling Melissa that it was time for her to move on to the high spiritual teachings of ECK. She had graduated from the primary schools of religion. Now it was time to return home to God.

Past lives, dreams, and Soul Travel are all part of Eckankar. They can help open your spiritual ears to the divine love that surrounds you every minute of every day.

Look into the ECK teachings. You will find they are charged with the energy of life and love. Those qualities can be yours too.

Today.

Glossary

Words set in SMALL CAPS are defined elsewhere in this glossary.

ARAHATA. An experienced and qualified teacher for ECKANKAR classes.

CHELA. A spiritual student.

ECK. The Life Force, the Holy Spirit, or Audible Life Current which sustains all life.

ECKANKAR. Religion of the Light and Sound of God. Also known as the Ancient Science of SOUL TRAVEL. A truly spiritual religion for the individual in modern times, known as the secret path to God via dreams and SOUL TRAVEL. The teachings provide a framework for anyone to explore their own spiritual experiences. Established by Paul Twitchell, the modern-day founder, in 1965.

ECK MASTERS. Spiritual Masters who can assist and protect people in their spiritual studies and travels. The ECK Masters are from a long line of God-Realized SOULS who know the responsibility that goes with spiritual freedom.

HU. The most ancient, secret name for God. The singing of the word HU, pronounced like the word *hue,* is considered a love song to God. It is sung in the ECK Worship Service.

INITIATION. Earned by the ECK member through spiritual unfoldment and service to God. The initiation is a private ceremony in which the individual is linked to the Sound and Light of God.

LIVING ECK MASTER. The title of the spiritual leader of ECKANKAR. His duty is to lead SOULS back to God. The Living ECK Master can assist spiritual students physically as the Outer Master, in the dream state as the Dream Master, and in the spiritual worlds as the Inner Master. Sri Harold Klemp became the MAHANTA, the Living ECK Master in 1981.

MAHANTA. A title to describe the highest state of God Consciousness on earth, often embodied in the LIVING ECK MASTER. He is the Living Word.

PLANES. The levels of heaven, such as the Astral, Causal, Mental, Etheric, and Soul planes.

SATSANG. A class in which students of ECK study a monthly lesson from ECKANKAR.

THE SHARIYAT-KI-SUGMAD. The sacred scriptures of ECKANKAR. The scriptures are comprised of twelve volumes in the spiritual worlds. The first two were transcribed from the inner PLANES by Paul Twitchell, modern-day founder of ECKANKAR.

SOUL. The True Self. The inner, most sacred part of each person. Soul exists before birth and lives on after the death of the physical body. As a spark of God, Soul can see, know, and perceive all things. It is the creative center of Its own world.

SOUL TRAVEL. The expansion of consciousness. The ability of SOUL to transcend the physical body and travel into the spiritual worlds of God. Soul Travel is taught only by the LIVING ECK MASTER. It helps people unfold spiritually and can provide proof of the existence of God and life after death.

SOUND AND LIGHT OF ECK. The Holy Spirit. The two aspects through which God appears in the lower worlds. People can experience them by looking and listening within themselves and through SOUL TRAVEL.

SPIRITUAL EXERCISES OF ECK. The daily practice of certain techniques to get us in touch with the Light and Sound of God.

SUGMAD. A sacred name for God. Sugmad is neither masculine nor feminine; It is the source of all life.

WAH Z. The spiritual name of Sri Harold Klemp. It means the Secret Doctrine. It is his name in the spiritual worlds.

Bibliography

"The Answer Man Can." *The Mystic World,* September 1995.

"Are Right and Wrong a Part of Spiritual Law?" *The Mystic World,* March 1994.

"Can You Ever Go Back?" *The Mystic World,* September 1992.

"Connecting Diamonds." *The Mystic World,* Winter 1991.

"Cry of the Hawk." *The Mystic World,* June 1993.

"Do You Love Me?" *The Mystic World,* Summer 1989.

"Dreams, Your Road to Heaven." *ECKANKAR Journal,* 1989.

"The ECK Researchers." *The Mystic World,* March 1995.

"The ECK Temple: A Gift to the World." *The Mystic World,* Winter 1990.

"The First ECK Initiations." *The Mystic World,* June 1992.

"Getting Answers from God through Past Lives, Dreams, and Soul Travel." *ECKANKAR Journal,* 1996.

"How God Speaks to Us, and How We Respond." *ECKANKAR Journal,* 1995.

"How Karma and Reincarnation Lead to Spiritual Freedom." *The Mystic World,* December 1993.

"How Your Dreams Can Help You Find Peace of Mind." *ECKANKAR Journal,* 1991.

"HU, the Age-Old Name for God." *The Mystic World,* Spring 1990.

"In Pursuit of God." *ECKANKAR Journal,* 1993.

"Kitchen-Table Conversations." *The Mystic World,* Summer 1990.

"Notes on Health and Healing." *The Mystic World,* June 1995.

"The Purpose of Dreams." *The Mystic World,* September 1994.

"A Quick Look at World Religions" ("Our First Twenty-five Years"). *The Mystic World,* Fall 1990.

"The Seat of Power." *The Mystic World,* Winter 1989.

"The Secret Side of ECK." *The Mystic World,* Spring 1991.

"Small as a Thimble?" *The Mystic World,* Spring 1989.

"Superman or Mickey Mouse?" *The Mystic World,* December 1995.

"The Temple of ECK." *The Mystic World,* Fall 1989.

"Tips on How to Interpret Your Dreams." *ECKANKAR Journal,* 1994.

"Treasures Lost and Found." *The Mystic World,* June 1994.

"Turning Points." *The Mystic World,* Spring 1992.

"The 12-Year Cycle." *The Mystic World,* December 1994.

"Use What You Are." *The Mystic World,* December 1992.

"What Is True Worship?" *The Mystic World,* Summer 1991.

"What We So Far Know of God." *ECKANKAR Journal,* 1992.

"Your Dreams—A Window to Heaven." *The Mystic World,* September 1993.

"Your Dreams and Graceful Living." *The Mystic World,* March 1993.

"Your Superstitions—How They Put You in a Box." *The Mystic World,* Fall 1991.

"Your Universe of Dreams." *ECKANKAR Journal,* 1990.

Index

231

232

Marriage
Religion(s) (religious). *See also*
    Buddha (Buddhism);
    Christian(s)(ity); Church;
    Eckankar; Hinduism; Islam;
    Judaism (Jews); Sikh
    religion; Sufis
    are of ECK, 2
    failings of, 189
    God doesn't support a certain,
        75
    has rules for living, 99
    immature, 48
    leaders, 2, 13, 209
    lifetimes in one, 47
    and Light and Sound. *See*
        Light and Sound of God: and
        other religions
    orthodox, 3, 175
    primary schools of, 219
    promises of, 46
    purpose of, 2
    relative unimportance of, 78
    review of major, 81 – 85
    and seat of power, 169
    talking about, 176
    writers, 3
Repetition, 211
Researchers, 200 – 201
Respect, 88, 176
Responsibility, 46, 77, 112, 196
Right and wrong, 99 – 100, 101
Rod of ECK Power, 157, 163,
    164, 189, 194
Role model(s), 210, 212
Roman Catholic(s), 89, 164, 172
    Church, 108
Roman Empire, 100, 170

Saint Paul, 172, 173. *See also*
    Saul of Tarsus
Saint(s), 9, 183
Salt, 22 – 23, 138
Salvation, 81
Sanctifier, 14
Satan, 3

Satsang. *See* Eckankar: Satsang
    class(es)
Saul of Tarsus, 9
Scriptures, 112, 165. *See also*
    Bible; *Shariyat-Ki-Sugmad,*
    The; Shariyat-Ki-Sugmad,
    the
Sculpture, 108
Seashell, 182
Seat of Power, 159, 160, 163,
    169 – 73
Seeker(s), 47, 200, 209, 210
Selected Fables, 131
Self(-). *See also* Self-Realization
    discipline, 139, 212
    higher. *See* Soul
    little, 210 – 11
    pity, 215
    service, 200
    sufficient, 212
Self-Realization, 120
Seminar
    Eckankar, 215
    1992 ECK European, 93
Senses, 182
Serve (serving) (service), 200
    ECK, 165
    God, 166, 196
    joy in, 194
    others, 112, 164
    out of love for God, 76 – 77
    ways of giving, 77
Sewing machine, 63
Shame, 144 – 47
Shariyat-Ki-Sugmad, The, 2,
    153, 165
Shariyat-Ki-Sugmad, the, 157,
    158
Sikh religion, 83
Sin, 45 – 46, 84
Skills, 212
Slave, 127
Society (social)
    acceptance, 204
    Christian, 99
    consciousness, 145

237

"Free Eckankar book reveals how to discover spiritual truth *through* past lives, dreams, and Soul Travel"

If you're serious about your quest for truth, you'll want to read *ECKANKAR—Ancient Wisdom for Today*. Hundreds of thousands of people around the globe have read it, and so many have benefited spiritually. A seeker from New York said, "I received your packet and read your book, which was extremely helpful to me. Thank you."

A Florida newspaper wrote that this book is "fascinating and well worth reading as you bring deeper spiritual insight into your life."

You'll see how **past lives** affect every aspect of your life. The way you handle relationships. Make choices. Face challenges.

You'll learn through your own personal experience that **dreams** are real. They help you make better decisions. Lose the fear of dying—and living—by understanding them.

Using a special technique, you'll find out how **Soul Travel** is a natural method for intuitively seeing the big picture, discovering spiritual truth. Begin the adventure of a lifetime *today*.

To request your free copy of *ECKANKAR—Ancient Wisdom for Today (a $4.95 value),* call

☎1-800-LOVE GOD
(1-800-568-3463)
toll free, 24 hours a day. Ask for book #942

Or write to ECKANKAR, Dept. 942,
P.O. Box 27300, Minneapolis, MN 55427 U.S.A.

Introductory Books on Eckankar

How the Inner Master Works
Mahanta Transcripts, Book 12
Harold Klemp

A woman decides to go back to work after being home for eleven years. After many rejections, she has a dream where the Inner Master helps her find just the right job.

This is just one of the many true stories Harold Klemp gives, along with thirty techniques, to help you find the Inner Master and take your next spiritual step.

ECKANKAR—Ancient Wisdom for Today

Are you one of the millions who have heard God speak through a profound spiritual experience? This introductory book will show you how dreams, Soul Travel, and experiences with past lives are ways God speaks to you. An entertaining, easy-to-read approach to Eckankar. Reading this little book can give you new perspectives on your spiritual life.

Ask the Master, Book 1
Harold Klemp

"What is my purpose in life?" "Are dreams real?" "How do past lives affect us today?" Harold Klemp, the spiritual leader of Eckankar, gives clear and candid answers to these and other questions he receives from people around the globe. His answers can help you overcome fear, learn self-discipline, be more creative, and improve family relationships.

HU: A Love Song to God
(Audiocassette)

Learn how to sing an ancient name for God, HU (pronounced like the word *hue*). A wonderful introduction to Eckankar, this two-tape set is designed to help listeners of any religious or philosophical background benefit from the gifts of the Holy Spirit. It includes an explanation of the HU, stories about how Divine Spirit works in daily life, and exercises to uplift you spiritually.

For fastest service, phone (612) 544-0066 weekdays between 8 a.m. and 5 p.m., central time, to request books using your credit card. Or write: **ECKANKAR, Att: Information, P.O. Box 27300, Minneapolis, MN 55427 U.S.A.**

There May Be an
Eckankar Study Group near You

Eckankar offers a variety of local and international activities for the spiritual seeker. With hundreds of study groups worldwide, Eckankar is near you! Many areas have Eckankar centers where you can browse through the books in a quiet, unpressured environment, talk with others who share an interest in this ancient teaching, and attend beginning discussion classes on how to gain the attributes of Soul: wisdom, power, love, and freedom.

Around the world, Eckankar study groups offer special one-day or weekend seminars on the basic teachings of Eckankar. Check your phone book under **ECKANKAR**, or call **(612) 544-0066** for membership information and the location of the Eckankar center or study group nearest you. Or write **ECKANKAR, Att: Information, P.O. Box 27300, Minneapolis, MN 55427 U.S.A.**

☐ Please send me information on the nearest Eckankar center or study group in my area.

☐ Please send me more information about membership in Eckankar, which includes a twelve-month spiritual study.

Please type or print clearly   940

Name _____
            first (given)   last (family)

Street_____ Apt. # _____

City _____ State/Prov. _____

ZIP/Postal Code _____ Country _____

About the Author

Sri Harold Klemp was born in Wisconsin and grew up on a small farm. He attended a two-room country schoolhouse before going to high school at a religious boarding school in Milwaukee, Wisconsin.

After preministerial college in Milwaukee and Fort Wayne, Indiana, he enlisted in the U.S. Air Force. There he trained as a language specialist at the University of Indiana and a radio intercept operator at Goodfellow AFB, Texas. Then followed a two-year stint in Japan where he first encountered Eckankar.

In October 1981, he became the spiritual leader of Eckankar, Religion of the Light and Sound of God. His full title is Sri Harold Klemp, the Mahanta, the Living ECK Master. As the Living ECK Master, Harold Klemp is responsible for the continued evolution of the Eckankar teachings.

His mission is to help people find their way back to God in this life. Harold Klemp travels to ECK seminars in North America, Europe, and the South Pacific. He has also visited Africa and many countries throughout the world, meeting with spiritual seekers and giving inspirational talks. There are many videocassettes and audiocassettes of his public talks available.

In his talks and writings, Harold Klemp's sense of humor and practical approach to spirituality have helped many people around the world find truth in their lives and greater inner freedom, wisdom, and love.

International Who's Who of Intellectuals
Ninth Edition

Reprinted with permission of Melrose Press Ltd., Cambridge, England, excerpted from *International Who's Who of Intellectuals, Ninth Edition,* Copyright 1992 by Melrose Press Ltd.

$$
\begin{array}{r}
2009 \\
\underline{1926} \\
83
\end{array}
$$